KT-382-641

The
Compact
Music
Dictionary

Driver and Vehicle
Licensing Agency

INS95

Important Notice
Plastic Wallets

DVLA no longer issue plastic wallets
with photocard driving licences.
This decision was taken primarily to
help minimise the administrative costs
of issuing licences to the public.
The Agency has also received
numerous complaints from members
of the public about the size of the
plastic wallet. Consequently, many
drivers discard the wallet and use
a different way of protecting their
licence.

**PLEASE NOTE: Old plastic wallets
sent in to the Agency cannot be
returned.**

*An executive agency of the
Department for*
Transport

The
Compact
Music
Dictionary

Over 2200 clear, concise definitions of musical terms
Pronunciations for all foreign terms

Amsco Publications
New York/London/Paris/Sydney

Compiled by Marilyn Bliss

Copyright © 1995 by Amsco Publications,
A Division of Music Sales Corporation, New York, NY.

All rights reserved. No part of this book may be
reproduced in any form or by any electronic or mechanical means
including information storage and retrieval systems,
without permission in writing from the publisher
except by a reviewer who may quote brief passages in a review.

Order No. AM 92225
US International Standard Book Number: 0.8256.1430.9
UK International Standard Book Number: 0.7119.4351.6

Exclusive Distributors:
Music Sales Corporation
257 Park Avenue South, New York, NY 10010 USA
Music Sales Limited
8/9 Frith Street, London W1V 5TZ England
Music Sales Pty. Limited
120 Rothschild Street, Rosebery, Sydney, NSW 2018, Australia

Printed in the United States of America by
Vicks Lithograph and Printing Corporation

Rules for Pronouncing
German, French, and Italian

The Vowels are often not pronounced as in English. The system of pronunciation employed in this Manual is explained below.

ah is the broad *a* in *father.*

ăh is a shorter version of the same sound; like *ah* in "rah! rah! rah!"

ă is the short English *a,* as in *bat.*

â is like *a* in *bare.*

ä is nearly like â, but closer. Short ä (ä̆) is nearly like *e* in *bet,* but more open.

ā is nearly like *a* in *bate;* only the long English *a* ends with a soft sound like short ĭ, called a "vanish," caused by slightly raising the root of the tongue (āⁱ); whereas the long "Continental" *a* has no vanish.

ĕh is the short sound of long *a* (closer than *e* in *bet*).

ĕ is short *e,* as in *bet.*

ē is long *e,* like *ee* in *beet.*

ī is long *i,* as in *bite.*

ĭ is short *i,* as in *bit,* though sometimes shaded towards *ee.*

oh is like *o* in *bode;* only the long English *o* ends with a soft sound like *u* in *bull,* called a "vanish," caused by drawing the lips together (ōᵘ); whereas the long "Continental" *o* has no vanish.

ŏh is short *o,* like the first *o* in *opinion.*

ŏ is the so–called broad Italian *o,* pronounced like *aw* in *law.*

ö is a sound not found in English. To pronounce long ö, set the lips as if to say "oh," and then say "ā" (as in *bate*), *keeping the lips fixed* in the first position; for short ö (ö̆) set the lips as before, but then say "ĕ" (as in *bet*), *keeping the lips fixed* in the first position.

oo is like long *oo* in *boot.*

ŏŏ is like short *oo* in *book.*

ŭ is short *u,* as in *but.*

ŭh is like the *u* in *fur.*

ü is a sound not found in English. To pronounce long ü, set the lips as if to say "oo" (as in *boot*), and then say "ee" (as in *beet*), *keeping the lips fixed* in the first position; for short ü (ü̆), set the lips as before, but then say "ĭ" (as in *bit*), *keeping the lips fixed* in the first position.

DIPHTHONGS:

ahü represents the German *äu* or *eu;* pronounce as one syllable quickly drawn together, accent on the "ah" (ah´ü). It is somewhat like the English *oy* in *boy* (aw´ĭ).

wăh represents the French *oi* ; pronounce as if written o‿äh, in one syllable quickly drawn together, accent on the "ah" (o‿äh´).

ow is like *ow* in *brow.*

5

THE CONSONANTS are usually pronounced as in English. The following signs need explanation:

yh represents a sound not found in English, namely, the *soft* German *ch*. Set the tongue as if to pronounce "ye," and then breathe (whisper) "he" through between tongue and hard palate (see ALLMÄHLICH).

h represents a sound not found in English, namely, the *hard* German *ch*. It is merely a rough breathing, as if one were trying gently to clear one's throat.

ng^k represents the sound *ng* at the end of German words, which finish, after the usual *ng* sound (*ng* as in *ring*), with a light *k* sound (See AUFFÜHRUNG).

n represents a sound not found in English, namely, the French nasal *n*. To get the correct nasal sound, the *n* must be pronounced, not *after* the vowel, but *together* with the vowel; that is, the vowel must be spoken through the nose, thus becoming a nasal vowel.

r is to be pronounced with a roll, tip of tongue against hard palate.

s must be pronounced *sharp*, wherever it occurs in the marked pronounciation; *soft* s is represented by z.

zh represents the *z* in *azure*.

The consonants *d* and *t* are usually formed, in the Continental languages, by touching the root of the upper front teeth with the tip of the tongue. To make this point clear, first pronounce the English word "dry" in the ordinary way, tip of tongue against the hard palate; then pronounce the German "drei," but taking the *dr* with tip of tongue against root of upper front teeth.—Form *t* in the same manner.

The German *w* is a compound of the English *w* and *v;* i.e., to get it right, the lips must almost close and, *at the same time*, the lower lip must lightly touch the upper front teeth.

N.B.—All accents (vowel marks) found on the entries, such as à, ä, â, é, è, ê, ö, ü, etc., belong to the words as correctly written in their respective languages.

A

A. 1. (Ger. *A;* Fr. and It., *La*). The sixth tone and degree in the typical diatonic scale of C major.—2. In music theory, capital *A* stands for the *A*-major triad, small *a* for the *a*-minor triad.—3. In Italian, *a* [ăh] (in French, *à* [ăh]) signifies to, at, for, by, in, etc.—4. In this Manual, an **-a** following an Italian word means that in the feminine form of the word **a** takes the place of the masculine ending **o**.

Ab (Ger., ăhp). Off (in organ music).

A B A. A symbolic representation for ternary form, in which the first statement (*A*) is repeated after (*B*). Most classical songs follow this formula. *A B A* is, therefore, also known as Song form. See SONG FORM.

A battuta (It., ăh băht-too′tăh). "With the beat"; in strict time.

Abbandono, con (It., kŏhn ăhb-băn-doh′nŏh). Yielding wholly to emotion; with a burst of passion; carried away by feeling.

Abbandonare (It., ăhb-băhn-dŏh-nah′rĕh). To abandon; quit; *senza abbandonare la corda*, without quitting the string.

Abbellimenti (It. ăhb-bĕl-lē-men′tē). Embellishments.

Abendmusik (Ger., ăhb-bend-moo-zĭk). Evening music.

Aber (Ger., ah′behr). But.

Abgemessen (Ger., ăhp′gĕ-mes′sen). Measured; in strict time.

Abgestossen (Ger., ăhp′gĕ-shtoh′sen). "Struck off"; detached; *staccato.*

Ablösen (Ger., ahb′lö-zen). To loosen; to separate one note from another.

Abnehmend (Ger., ăhp′nā′ment). *Diminuendo.*

Abschnitt (Ger., ahb′shnitt). Section.

Abschwellen (Ger., ăhp′shvel′len). *Decrescendo.*

Absetzen (Ger., ahb′zet-zen). To separate; to detach.

Absolute music. Music without extramusical connotation. Compare PROGRAM MUSIC.

Absolute pitch. Ability to name instantly and without fail any note struck on the piano keyboard or played on an instrument. This is an innate faculty, distinct from relative pitch, in which an interval is named in relation to a previously played note. Absolute pitch is also known as Perfect pitch.

Abstract music. A term often used for ABSOLUTE MUSIC.

A cappella (It., ăh căhp-pel′läh). "As in chapel," that is, as in the church style; choral singing without instrumental accompaniment.

Accelerando (It., ăht-chĕh-lĕh-rahn´dŏh). "Accelerating," growing faster.

Accent. A stress.

Acciaccatura (It., ăht-chăh-kăh-too´răh). 1. A short accented appoggiatura.—2. A note a second above, and struck with, the principal note, and instantly released.

Accidental. Any chromatic sign not found in the key signature, occurring in the course of a piece.

Accompagnato (It., ahk-kohm-pahn-yah´toh). 1. Accompanied.—2. A recitative with ensemble accompaniment.

Accompaniment. Any part or parts that attend the voices or instruments bearing the principal part or parts in a musical composition. It is *ad libitum* when the piece can be performed without it, and *obbligato* when it is necessary to the piece. . . *Additional accompaniments* are parts added to a composition by some other person than its original author.

Accopiato (It., ăhk-kŏp-pē-ăh´tŏh). Tied, bound.

Accord (Fr., ah-kor´). Chord.

Accordatura (It., ăhk-kor-dăh-too´răh). The "tuning," or series of tones according to which a string instrument is tuned; g-d^1-a^1-e^2 is the *accordatura* of the violin.

Accorder (Fr., ah-kor-day´). To tune.

Accordion. A free-reed instrument whose elongated body serves as a bellows; the bellows is closed at either end by a keyboard, that for the right hand having a diatonic scale, while that for the left hand has 2 or more keys for harmonic bass tones. See CONCERTINA.

Accoupler (Fr., ahk-koo-play´). "To couple," as in organ playing.

Achtelnote (Ger., ah´-tel-no´-tay). Eighth note.

Acoustics. The science of sound.

Action. In keyboard instruments, the mechanism set in motion by the player's fingers, or by the feet (organ pedals).—In the harp, the "action" (a set of pedals) does not directly produce the sound, but changes the key by shortening the strings by a semitone or whole tone.

Acute. High in pitch, sharp, shrill; opposed to Grave.

Adagietto (It., ăh-dăh-jet´tŏh). 1. A movement slightly faster than Adagio.—2. A short Adagio.

Adagio (It., ăh-dăh´jŏh). Slow, leisurely; a slow movement. . . *Adagio assai, adagio molto,* very slow. . . *Adagio non molto,* or *non tanto,* not too slow.

Adagissimo (It., ăh-dăh-jis´sē-mŏh). Extremely slow.

Added seventh. A minor or major seventh added to the concluding major triad.

Added sixth. A sixth added to the major tonic triad, usually at the end of a phrase, and treated as a consonance.

Addolorato (It., ăhd-dŏh-lŏh-rah′tŏh). Plaintive; in a style expressing grief.

À demi-jeu (Fr., ăh-dŭ-mē-zhö′). With half the power of the instrument.

À demi-voix (Fr., ăh-dŭ-mē-vwăh′). MEZZA VOCE.

À deux (Fr., ăh dö′). A DUE; *à deux mains*, for two hands.

Ad libitum (L., ăhd lĭ′bi-tŭm, "at will"). A direction signifying (1) that the performer may choose the tempo or expression; (2) that any part so marked may be left out, if desired. *Cadenza ad libitum* means that a given cadenza may be performed or not, or another substituted for it, at the performer's pleasure.

A due (It., ăh doo′ĕh). See DUE.

A dur (Ger., ah door′). *A* major.

Aeolian harp. A string instrument sounded by the wind. It is a narrow, oblong, wooden box with low bridges, across which are stretched gut strings.

Aeolian mode. A mode beginning on the sixth degree of the major scale, as in *A, B, C, D, E, F, G, A.*

Affabile (It., ăhf-fah′bē-lĕh). Sweetly and gracefully; suavely.

Affannoso (It., ăhf-făh-nŏh′sŏh). Anxious, restless.

Affettuoso (It., ăhf-fet-tŏŏ-oh′sŏh). With feeling; very expressively; tenderly.

Afflitto (It., ăhf-flēt′tŏh). Melancholy, sad.

Affrettato (It., ăhf-fret-tah′tŏh). Hurried; *tempo piu affrettato*, at a swifter pace.

Agevole (It., ăh-jā′vŏh-lĕh). Easy, light.

Aggiustatamente (It., ăh-jŏŏs-tăh-tăh-men′-tĕh). Strictly in time.

Agiatamente (It., ăh-jăh-tăh-men′tĕh). Easily, indolently.

Agilmente (It., ăh-jēl-men′tĕh). Lightly, vivaciously.

Agitatamente (It., ăh-jē-tăh-tăh-men′tĕh). Excitedly, agitatedly.

Agitato (It., ăh-jē-tah′tŏh). Agitated. . . *Agitato con passione,* passionately agitated.

Agogic. A relatively modern term, from the Greek verb "to lead," applied to slight deviations from the main rhythm.

Agréments (Fr., ah-grā-mahn′). Plural noun for ornaments used in Baroque music.

Ai (It., ah′ē). See ALL′.

Air. A tune or melody.

Ais (Ger., ah′iss). *A* sharp.

Aisis (Ger., ah′iss-iss). *A* double sharp.

À l'aise (Fr., ah lehz′). "At ease"; in a relaxed manner.

À la mesure (Fr. ăh lăh mŭ-zŭr′). In strict time.

Alberti bass. A bass in broken chords, like

Alborada (Sp., ăhl-bŏ-răh′-dăh). Type of Spanish music; originally a morning serenade. See AUBADE.

Album-leaf, Ger. **Albumblatt** (ăhl′-bŭm-blăht). Title of a short and (usually) simple vocal or instrumental piece.

Alcuno, -a (It., ăhl-koo′nŏh, -năh). Some; certain. . . *Con alcuna licenza,* "with a certain freedom" (as regards tempo).

Aleatory. A modern word as applied to music, from the Latin *alea,* "a game of dice." In Aleatory music, rhythmic values, pitch, dynamics, duration all may be subject to multiple choices by the performer. In extreme cases even the length of the piece itself is aleatory. Aleatory music is sometimes called *chance music.*

Al fine (It., ăhl fē-něh). "To the finish"; used in phrases such as *Dal segno al fine,* "from the sign to the end marked *Fine.*"

All', Alla (It., ăhl, ăhl′-lăh). To the, in the, at the, etc.; in the style of, like.

Alla breve (It., — brâ′věh). $\mathbf{\phi}$ In modern music, a meter of $\frac{2}{2}$; i.e., two beats per measure with the half note carrying the beat; also called "cut time." The implication is of a faster tempo than $\frac{4}{4}$.

Alla caccia (It. — căht′chăh). In the hunting style.

Alla marcia (It., — mahr′chăh). In march style.

Allargando (It., ăhl-lar-gähn′dŏh). Growing slower.

Allagare, senza (It., sen′tsăh ăhl-lar-gah′rěh). Without slackening speed.

Alla russa (It., ăhl′-lăh rŏŏs′săh). In the Russian style.

Alla stretta (It., — strě′tăh). 1. Growing faster and faster.—2. In the style of a Stretta *(or Stretto).*

Alla turca (It., — toor′kăh). In Turkish style.

Alla veneziana (It., — věh-něh-tsē-ah′năh). In the Venetian style (like a Gondoliera).

Alla zingara (It., — tsin′gäh-răh). In the style of Gypsy music.

Alla zoppa (It., — tsôp′păh). Lamely, haltingly; in syncopated style.

Allegrettino (It., ăhl-lĕh-gret-tē′nŏh). 1. A short Allegretto movement.—2. A tempo slower than Allegretto.

Allegretto (It., ăhl-lĕh-gret′tŏh). Quite lively; moderately fast (faster than Andante, slower than Allegro).

Allegrissimo (It., ăhl-lĕh-gris′sē-mŏh). Very rapidly.

Allegro (It., ăhl-lā′grŏh). Lively, brisk, rapid. Allegro is not quite as fast as Presto. . . *Allegro assai, Allegro di molto,* very fast.

Allegro ma non troppo (It., ăhl-lā′grŏh măh nŏhn trŏp′pŏh). "Fast, but not too much."

Allein (Ger., ăhl-līn′). Alone; only.

Alleluia. The Latin form of Hallelujah (Praise the Lord!).

Allemande (Fr., ăhl-l′-mahn′d). 1. A German dance in ¾ time, like the LÄNDLER.—2. A lively German dance in ²⁄₄ time.—3. A movement in the Baroque suite in ⁴⁄₄ time and moderate tempo (*andantino*).

Allentato (It., ăhl-len-tah′tŏh). Slower.

Allmählich (Ger., ăhl-mä′lĭyh). Gradually, by degrees.

Al loco (It., ăhl lô′kŏh). A direction following "8va," meaning "perform as written."—Also directs a violinist to return to a former position after a shift.

Allongé (Fr., ăhl′lŏhn-zhā′). Prolonged stroke (of the bow).

Allora (It., ăhl-loh′răh). Then.

All' ottava (It., ăhl ŏht-tah′văh). "At the octave"; meaning, "play the notes an octave higher than written." The sign 8va ----- or 8 ----- is usually employed.

All' unisono (It., ăhl oo-nē′sŏh-nŏh). In unison (or octaves).

Alma, con (It., kŏhn ăhl′măh). With soul, spirit; loftily; ardently.

Alphorn. A long Swiss trumpet used by shepherds in the Alps to call sheep home.

Al segno (It., ăhl sen′yoh). "To the sign," directing the performer to go on playing until the sign in the form of the large letter S superimposed on a large X.

Alt (from the It., *alto*). Notes "in alt" are those of the next octave above f^2. Notes in the octave higher than this are said to be "in altissimo."

Alt (Ger., ăhlt). Alto (voice or part).

Altered chords. Chords containing chromatic alterations of chords properly belonging to the tonality of the music; also called *chromatic chords.*

Alterezza (It., ăhl-tĕh-ret′săh). Pride, loftiness.

Alternativo (It., ăhl-târ-năh-tē′voh). Alternative, or rather a contrasting section in dance forms, such as a trio in a minuet.

Altieramente (It., ăhl-tē-ĕh-răh-men′tĕh). In a lofty, majestic style.

Altissimo (It., ăhl-tis′sē-mŏ-h). Highest. See ALT.

Alto (from the It., *alto*). 1. The deeper of the two main divisions of women's or boys' voices, the Soprano being the higher. (Also called *Contralto*.) Ordinary compass from *g* to *c²*.—2. An instrument of similar compass.—3. The countertenor voice.—4. The viola, or tenor violin.

Alto, -a (It., ăhl′tŏh, -tăh). High. . . *Alta viola*, tenor violin. . . *Ottava alta*, an octave higher.

Alto clef. A *C*-clef on the 3rd line.

Altro, -a (It., ăhl′trŏh, -trăh). Other. . . *Altri, Altre*, others.

Alzando (It., ăhl-tsăhn′dŏh). Raising. . . *Alzando un po′ la voce*, raising the voice a little.

Am (Ger., ăhm). By the.

Amabile (It., ăh-mah′bē-lĕh). Sweet, tender, gentle.

Amarevole (It., ăh-mah-rā′vŏh-lĕh). Bitterly; mournfully, grievingly.

Amaro (It., ăh-măh′-rŏh). Grief, bitterness.

Ambrosian chant. The system of liturgical singing connected with the practice established by St. Ambrose in the 4th century. Its structure is much freer than that of Gregorian chant, which followed two centuries later.

Amen. The concluding word in a Jewish or Christian prayer, which means "so be it." Sometimes an Amen section in an oratorio is extended so as to become a concluding chorus of considerable length.

A mezza voce (It., ăh med′zăh voh′chĕh). With half the power.

A moll (Ger., ah mŏhl′). *A* minor.

Amorevole (It., ăh-mŏh-rā-vŏh-lĕh). Amorously; lovingly, fondly, devotedly, tenderly.

Amoroso (It., ăh-mŏh-roh′sŏh). Amorous; loving, fond.

Anacrusis (Gk., ăn-ŭ-kroo′sĭs). One or two unaccented syllables beginning a verse of poetry. In music, the weak beat, or weak part of a measure, with which a piece or phrase may begin. See AUFTAKT.

Anapest. A metrical foot of 3 syllables, 2 short and 1 long: ˘ ˘ ‒.

Anche (Fr., ăhnsh). Reed. . . *Jeu d'anches* [zhö dăhnsh], reed stop.

Ancora (It., ăhn-koh′răh). Again, still, even. . . *Ancora più mosso*, still faster. . . *Ancora piano*, continue singing or playing softly. . . *Ancora più piano*, still more softly.

Andacht, mit (Ger., mit ăhn′dăht). With devotion; devoutly.

Andamento (It., ăhn-dăh-men′-tŏh). "Going"; an energetic tempo.

Andante (It., ăhn-dăhn′tĕh). "Going," "moving"; a tempo mark indicating a moderately slow, easily flowing movement between Adagio and Allegretto. —*Andante cantabile*, flowingly, in a singing style. . . *A. con moto, A. mosso, A. un poco allegretto*, a flowing and rather more animated movement. . . *A. non troppo*, easily flowing, but not too fast.

Andantino (It., ăhn-dăhn-tē′nŏh). A diminutive of Andante, meaning, properly, a little slower than *andante*; but often used as if meaning a little faster.

Andare (It., ăhn-dah′rĕh). To move on. . . *Andare diritto*, go straight on. . . *Andare in tempo*, keep strict time.

Anfang (Ger., ăhn′făhngᵏ). Beginning. . . *Vom Anfang*, same as DA CAPO.

Angemessen (Ger., ăhn′gĕ-mĕssen). Suitable, comfortable.

Angenehm (Ger., ăhn′gĕ-nāhm). Pleasing, agreeable.

Angklung. A Javanese tube made of bamboo, and included in a gamelan ensemble.

Anglican chant. Liturgical singing in the Anglican Church, usually harmonized with simple chords.

Angoscioso (It., ăhn-gŏh-shŏh′sŏh). With anguish, with mental agony.

Ängstlich (Ger., engst′lĭyh). Anxiously, fearfully.

Anhang (Ger., ăhn′hăhngᵏ). Coda, codetta.

Animando (It., ăh-nē-mahn′dŏh). With increasing animation.. . *Lo stesso tempo e animando sempre più*, the same rate of speed, with ever increasing animation.

Animoso (It., ăh-nē-moh′sŏh). Animated, spirited.

Anlaufen (Ger., ăhn′low-fen). To increase in volume.

Anmut(h)ig (Ger., ăhn′moo′tĭyh). With grace, charm; gracefully, suavely.

Anschlag (Ger., ăhn′shlă′h). 1. The TOUCH in piano playing.—2. An ornament.—3. A stroke, or the striking of a chord.

Anschwellen (Ger., ăhn′shvel′len). To swell, become louder.

Anschwellend (Ger., —lent). *Crescendo*.

Ansioso (It., ăhn-sē-oh′sŏh). In a style expressive of anxiety or hesitation.

Anstimmen (Ger., ăhn′shtĭm-men). To tune, to begin to sing.

Anstimmung (Ger., ăhn´shtĭm-moongᵏ). Tuning, intonation.

Answer. In a fugue, the taking-up by the *second* part (at a different pitch) of the subject proposed by the *first* part.

Antecedent. The theme or subject of a canon or fugue, as proposed by the first part; the Leader.

Anthem. A piece of sacred choral music usually founded on biblical words, with or without instrumental accompaniment, and of moderate length.

Anticipation. The advancing of one or more of the parts constituting a harmony before the rest; which would, if all the parts progressed together, enter later.

Antico (It., ăhn-tē´kŏh). Antique, ancient. . . *All' antico*, in the ancient style.

Antiphon. Originally, a responsive system of singing by two choirs (or divided choir), an early feature in the Catholic song service; later applied to responsive or alternate singing, chanting, or intonation in general.

Antiphonal. 1. A book or collection of antiphons or anthems.—2. In the style of an antiphon; responsive, alternating.

Antiphony. Responsive singing by two choirs (or divided choir) or alternate verses of a psalm or anthem.

Antique cymbal. A very small pair of brass cymbals, such as were used in accompanying dances in ancient Greece; sometimes used in modern scores.

Anvil. A metal bar used as a percussion instrument for special effects, as in the Anvil Chorus in Verdi's opera *Il Trovatore*.

Anwachsend (Ger., ăhn´văhk´sent). *Crescendo.*

Aperto (It., ăh-pâr´tŏh). Open, without a mute. . . *Allegro aperto*, an Allegro with broad, clear phrasing.

A piacere (It., ah pee-ah-cher´-eh). "As you please"; free in tempo and dynamics.

Appassionato, -a (It., ăhp-păhs-sē-ŏh-năh´tŏh, -tăh). Impassioned, with passion.

Appena (It., ăhp-pā´năh). Scarcely. . . *Appena animando*, a bit more animated. . . *Appena meno*, a very little slower. . . *Appena sensibile*, hardly audible.

Appenato (It., ăhp-pĕh-nah´tŏh). Distressed; in a style expressive of suffering.

Appoggiando (It., ăhp-pŏhd-jähn´dŏh). "Leaning on," "supported." Said of a tone gliding over to the next without a break, like an appoggiatura or portamento.

Appoggiatura (It., ăhp-pŏhd-jäh-too′răh). An *accented appoggiatura* is a grace note which takes the accent and part of the time value of the *following* principal note. The long appoggiatura

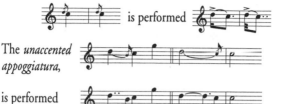

is seldom written now; the *short appoggiatura*

is performed

The *unaccented appoggiatura*,

is performed

taking its time value from the *preceding* principal note, to which it is bound.

A quattro mani (It., ăh kwăht′trŏh mah′nē). For 4 hands; keyboard duets.

A quattro voci (It., ăh kwăht′trŏh voh′chē). For 4 voices or parts.

Arabesque. A type of fanciful piano piece; ornamental passages accompanying or varying a theme.

Arcato (It., ar-kah′tŏh). With the bow.

Arch- (Engl.), **Arci-** (It., ar′chē). A prefix signifying "chief, pre-eminent," formerly applied to instruments in the sense of "largest," and to official titles in the sense of "head." *Archchanter*, precentor. . . *Archlute*, a large bass lute.

Arco (It., ar′kŏh). Bow. . .*Arco in giù* (joo′), down-bow; *arco in su* (soo′), up-bow.

Ardente (It., ar-den′tĕh). Ardent, fiery, passionate.

Ardito (It., ar-dē′tŏh). Bold, spirited.

Aria (It., ah′rē-äh). An air, song, tune, melody. The *grand* or *da capo aria* is in 3 divisions: (1) The theme, fully developed; (2) a more tranquil and richly harmonized section; (3) a repetition *da capo* of the first, with more florid ornamentation.

Aria buffa (It., — bŏŏf′fäh). A comic or burlesque aria.

Arietta (It., ah-rē-et′täh). A short air or song; a short aria.

Arioso (It., ăh-rē-oh′sŏh). In vocal music, a style between aria and recitative; or a short melodious strain interrupting or ending a recitative.—Also, an impressive, dramatic style suitable for the *aria grande*; hence, a vocal piece in that style.—In instrumental music, the same as *cantabile*.

Arpa (It., ar′pah). Harp.

Arpeggiando (It., ar-ped-jähn′dŏh). Playing in harp-style; sounding broken chords.

Arpeggio (It., ar-ped′jŏh). Playing the tones of a chord in rapid, even succession; playing broken chords. Hence, a chord so played; a broken or chord passage.

Arrangement. The adaptation of a composition for performance on an instrument, or by any vocal or instrumental combination, for which it was not originally written.

Ars antiqua (L., ahrz ăn-tē′kwŭ). A contrapuntal style of 12th-13th-century France.

Arsis and thesis (Gk., ahr′sēs, thēs′ēs). Upbeat and downbeat.

Ars nova (L. ahrz nō-vŭ, "new art"). The period of 14th-century music which contrasted with the Ars antiqua by its more complex counterpoint.

Articolato (It. ar-tē-kŏh-lah′tŏh). "Articulated"; *ben articolato*, clearly and neatly pronounced and phrased.

Artificial harmonics. Harmonics produced on a *stopped* rather than open string.

As (Ger., ăhss). A♭ (*A* flat).

Asas, or **Ases** (Ger., ăhss′ăhss, ăhss′ess). *A* double flat.

As dur (Ger., —dōōr). A♭ major.

Assai (It., ăhs-sah′ē). Very. . . *Allegro assai*, very fast. . . *Adagio assai*, very slow.

Assez (Fr., ăhs-sā′). Enough; rather.

A string. The 2nd string of a violin; the 1st of a viola, or 'cello; the 3rd of a double bass; the 5th of a guitar.

Atempause (Ger., ah′tŭm-powze). Literally, "breath-pause"; a slight break to catch the breath before a strong beat.

A tempo (It., ăh tem′pŏh). In time; at the preceding rate of speed.

Atonality. The absence of tonality. A type of modern music in which the traditional tonal structures are abandoned, and the key signature is absent.

Attaca (It., ăht-tăhk′kăh). "Attack" or begin what follows without pausing, or with a very short pause. . . *Attacca subito*, attack instantly.

Attack. The act (or style) of beginning a phrase, passage, or piece.

Attendant keys. Of a given key are its relative major or minor, together with the keys of the dominant and subdominant and their relative major or minor keys.

Attenzione, con (It., kŏhn ăht-ten-tsē-oh′nĕh). "With attention"; in a marked style.

Aubade (Fr., ōh-băhd). Morning music.

Aufführung (Ger., owf′füh-rŏŏng^k). Performance.

Aufgeregt (Ger., owf′-gĕ-rayht′). Agitated, excited.

Aufstrich (Ger., owf′strĭyh). An up bow.

Auftakt (Ger., owf'tăhkt). Upbeat, anacrusis; a fractional measure beginning a movement, piece, or theme.

Auftritt (Ger., owf'trĭtt). A scene of an opera.

Aufzug (Ger., owf'zŭg). An act of an opera.

Augmentation. Doubling (or increasing) the time value of the notes of a theme or motive in imitative counterpoint.

Augmented fourth. The interval a semitone bigger than the perfect fourth.

Augmented second. An interval a semitone larger than a major second.

Augmented sixth. An interval a semitone larger than a major sixth. It is the basic interval of the so-called French Sixth, German Sixth, and Italian Sixth.

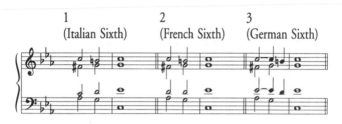

Augmented triad. A triad consisting of 2 major thirds, as in *C, E, G* sharp.

Aulos. An ancient Greek wind instrument resembling an oboe. It usually had two connected pipes, blown simultaneously.

Ausdruck (Ger., ows'drŏŏk). Expression.

Ausgabe (Ger., ows'găhbe). Edition.

Auszug (Ger., ows'tsŭh). Arrangement or reduction.

Authentic cadence. See CADENCE.

Authentic mode. A church mode in which the keynote is the lowest tone.

Autoharp. A zither-like educational instrument having devices for playing preset chords; used to demonstrate harmonic progressions and to accompany songs.

Auxiliary note. A note not essential to the harmony or melody; particularly, a grace note a second above or below a given melody note.

Auxiliary scales. Those of attendant keys.

Avec (Fr., ăh-vĕk'). With. . . *Avec âme* [ahm], the same as *con anima.*

Avoided cadence. See CADENCE.

Ayre. A 16th-17th-century English court song, usually accompanied on the lute.

B

B. 1. (Ger. *H*; Fr. and It., *si*). The seventh tone and degree in the diatonic scale of *C* major.—2. In music theory, capital *B* designates the *B*-major triad, small *b* the *b*-minor triad.—3. In German, *B* stands for *B♭*.—4. *B.* is also an abbreviation for *Bass* or *Basso* (*c. B.* = col Basso; *B. C.* = basso continuo).

Baby grand. The smallest size of the grand piano.

B-A-C-H. These letters of Bach's name represent in German nomenclature the notes *B* flat, *A*, *C*, and *B* natural. Bach used this chromatically sounding theme in the unfinished last fugue of his work *The Art of the Fugue*, and many subsequent composers have paid tribute to him by writing pieces based on the same 4 notes.

Backfall. A grace note, played like an accented appoggiatura.

Backturn. A melodic ornament that begins on a lower note.

Badinage (Fr., băh-di-nă′zh), also **Badinerie** (Fr., bah-dee-neh-ree′). Teasing, bantering; used in Baroque music as the title of a quick movement in $\frac{2}{4}$ time.

Bagatelle. A trifle; usually a short, fairly easy piece.

Bagpipe. An ancient wind instrument of Eastern origin. The most common form has 4 pipes, 3 drones (single-reed pipes tuned to a given tone, its fifth, and its octave, respectively; and sounding continuously), and 1 chanter or melody-pipe (a double-reed pipe with 6 or 8 holes), on which the tune is played. The "bag" is a leather sack, filled with wind from the mouth or from small bellows worked by the player's arm; the pipes are inserted in and receive wind from the bag.

Baguette (Fr., bah-get′). Conductor's baton; also a drumstick.

Baile (Sp. bi′-leh). A dance.

Balalaika. (Russian, băl-a-lī′kăh). Popular Russian instrument of the guitar type.

Ballad. Originally, a song intended for a dance accompaniment; hence, the air of such a song.—In modern usage, a ballad is a simple narrative poem, generally meant to be sung.—As a purely musical term, it was originally applied to a short, simple vocal melody, set to one or more stanzas, with a slight instrumental accompaniment. It now includes instrumental melodies of a similar character.

Ballade (Ger., băhl-lah′dĕ; Fr., băhl-lăhd′). A ballad-like art song, or an instrumental solo piece.

Ballad opera. An opera chiefly made up of ballads and folk songs.

Ballata (It., băhl-lah′tăh). A ballad.—*A ballata*, in ballad style.

Ballet (băl-lay′). 1. A staged dance, either independent or introduced in an opera or other stage-piece.—2. A pantomime, with music and dance setting forth the thread of the story.

Balletto (It., băhl-let′tŏh). 1. A Renaissance Italian dance.—2. A Renaissance Italian vocal piece.

Ballo (It., băhl′lŏh). A dance; a ballet.

Band. 1. A company of musicians playing martial music (brass band, military band).—2. An orchestra.—3. A section of the orchestra playing instruments of the same class.

Bandola (Sp., băhn-doh′lăh). [Also the *Bandolon, Bandora, Bandura*]. Instruments of the lute family, with a greater or smaller number of steel or gut strings, and played with a plectrum ("pick"); similar to the Mandolin.

Banjo. American folk instrument of African origin with 5 strings, which are plucked by the fingers or a pick.

Bar. A vertical line dividing measures on the staff, and indicating that the strong beat falls on the following note .—2. The informal name for "measure" (the notes and rests contained between two bars).

Barbershop harmony. A type of close harmony, often with chromatic passing notes, popular in America at the turn of the century.

Barcarola (It., bar-kăh-rô′lăh), **Barcarole** (Ger., bar-kăh-roh′lĕ), **Barcarolle** (Fr., bar-kăh-rŏhl′). 1. A gondoliera; song of the Venetian gondoliers.—2. A solo or concerted piece, imitating the Venetian boat songs, and usually in $\frac{6}{8}$ time.

Bariolage (Fr., băh-rē-ŏh-lăh′zh). A group of several notes played in the same position on 2, 3, or 4 violin strings.

Baritone. 1. The male voice between bass and tenor, and more or less similar in quality to both. Compass from G to f^1. Also, a singer having such a voice.—2. A bowed instrument like the *viola da gamba*.—3. The Euphonium.

Baritone clef. The obsolete F clef on the *third* line:

Baroque music. The type of contrapuntal music developed within the historical period of about 1600–1750. Bach and Handel belonged to this era. Although the word "Baroque" originally implied a bizarre and even crude quality, it has acquired the opposite meaning of dignity and precise craftsmanship.

Baroque suite. See CLASSICAL SUITE.

Barré (Fr., bar-rā′). In lute or guitar playing, the stopping of several or all strings with the left-hand forefinger.—*Grand* [grähn] *barré*, a stop of more than 3 strings.

Barrel organ. A type of mechanical organ. The Orchestrion is a large barrel organ.

Bass. 1. The lowest tone in a chord, or the lowest part in a composition.—2. The lowest male voice; ordinary compass from F to c^1.

Bass (Ger., bähs). Besides the English meanings above, denotes (a) an old bowed instrument between 'cello and double bass, with 5 or 6 strings; (b) the same as *Kontrabass* (double bass); (c) at the end of the name of an organ stop, it means that the stop is on the pedal (for example, *Gemshornbass*).

B

Bass-bar. In violins, a long narrow strip of wood glued to the belly parallel with and just beneath the *G*-string, used to strengthen the belly and equalize vibration.

Bass clef. *F* clef on the 4th line:

Basse danse. (Fr., băhs dähns). A medieval French dance.

Basset horn. A tenor clarinet of mellow timbre, with a compass from *F* to c^3.

Basso (It., băhs´sŏh). Bass; also, the double bass.

Basso buffo (It., —bŏŏf´fŏh). A comic bass.

Basso cantante (It., —kăhn-tăhn´tĕh). A bass-baritone.

Basso continuo (It., —kŏhn-tē´nŏŏ-ŏh). In Baroque ensemble music, the part played by a keyboard instrument and a low string or wind instrument.

Bassoon. A double-reed woodwind instrument; the double tube bears the long, curving, metallic mouthpiece. Compass from B_1b to f^2. Tone soft and mellow.

Basso ostinato (It., băhs´sŏh ŏh-stĕ-nah´tŏh). See GROUND BASS.

Basso profondo (It., — prō-fōhn´dŏh). "Profound bass"; the lowest bass voice.

Basstuba (Ger., băhs´too´băh). See TUBA 2.

Baton. A conductor's stick.

Battery (also Fr., **batterie**). 1. The group of percussion instruments.— 2. A drum roll.—3. 18th-century term for broken chord figures.

Battuta (It., băht-tŏŏ´-tăh). Beat; downbeat; measure. . . *A battuta*, in strict time.

B dur (Ger., bā door). *B* flat major.

Be (Ger., bā). The flat sign (♭).

Beat. 1. A movement of the hand in marking ("beating") time.—2. A division of a measure marked by a beat.—3. In a trill, the pulsation of 2 consecutive tones.—4. An appoggiatura.—5. A throbbing caused by the interfering tone waves of 2 tones of different pitch.

Bebop. A type of JAZZ that flourished in the 1940s–50s; associated with Charlie Parker and Dizzy Gillespie.

Bebung (Ger., beh´boong). "Trembling"; a vibrato effect on string instruments or the clavichord.

Bécarre (Fr., beh-car´). Natural sign (♮).

Becken (Ger., bek´en). Cymbal (singular); cymbals (plural).

Begleitung (Ger., bĕ-glī´tŏŏng^k). Accompaniment.

Bel canto (It., bel kăhn´tŏh). The art of beautiful song, as exemplified by Italian singers of the 18th–19th centuries. Opposed to Recitative, and to the "declamatory" style of singing brought into prominence by Wagner.

Belebt (Ger., bĕ-lāpt´). Animated, brisk.

Bell. A hollow metallic percussion instrument, sounded by a clapper hanging inside or a hammer outside.—Also, the flaring end of various wind instruments.

Bell harp. A kind of dulcimer used in 18th-century England.

Belly. The face (upper side) of the resonance box of the violin, etc.—Also, the soundboard of the piano.

Bémol (Fr., bā-mŏl). The flat sign (♭).

Bene (It., bâ´nĕh). [Abbreviation, *ben.*]. Well. . . *Ben marcato,* well marked; *a bene placito,* at pleasure; *ben sostenuto, ben tenuto,* well sustained.

Benedictus. In Latin, "blessed"; the concluding portion of the Sanctus in the Mass.

Berceuse (Fr., bâr-söz´). A cradle song, lullaby.

Bergerette (Fr., bâr-zhâr-et´). A pastoral or rustic song; also a type of 18th- century French lyrical poetry.

Beruhigend (Ger., bĕ-roo´-ĭyhent). Becoming calm.

Beschleunigen (Ger., bĕ-shlähü´nĭ-gen). To hasten.

Bestimmt (Ger., bĕ-shtimt´). With decision, energy.

Betont (Ger., bĕ-tohnt´). Accented, marked.

Bewegt (Ger., bĕ-vāyht´). Moved, agitated.

Bewegung (Ger., bĕ-vā´gŏŏng^k). Movement; agitation.

Bicinium. A composition for 2 voices or instruments.

Binary. Dual; two-part. . . *Binary form,* a form of movement founded on two principal themes (see SONATA), or divided into 2 distinct or contrasted sections.

Bind. 1. A tie.—2. A brace.

Bis. Twice; commonly used in Europe to request an encore. Also used in printed music to indiciate that a passage is to be repeated.

Biscroma. In Italian, a thirty-second note.

Bitonality. Harmony in 2 different tonalities, played simultaneously.

Blasinstrumente (Ger., blaz´in-stru-men-teh). Wind instruments.

Blech (Ger., bleh). Brass; *Blechmusik,* brass music.

Blockflöte (Ger., blŏhk´flö´tĕ). Recorder.

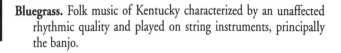

Block. In violins, etc., the blocks are small pieces of wood within the body, glued vertically to the ribs between belly and back to strengthen the instrument.

Bluegrass. Folk music of Kentucky characterized by an unaffected rhythmic quality and played on string instruments, principally the banjo.

Blue note. The lowered third and seventh degree in a major scale, as *B* flat and *E* flat in the *C* major scale; the blue note is characteristic in the blues and jazz.

Blues. An American ballad of black origins. It is in $\frac{4}{4}$ time, has a melody characterized by lowered third and seventh ("blue") notes, and has a standard 12- measure harmonic pattern.

B moll (Ger., bā mŏhl′). *B* flat minor.

Bocca (It., bŏhk′kăh). Mouth. . . *(Con) bocca chiusa* [kew′-săh], with closed mouth; humming. See BRUMMSTIMMEN.

Body. 1. The resonance box of a string instrument.—2. That part of a wind instrument remaining when mouthpiece, crooks, and bell are removed.

Boehm system. A system of playing the flute with keys replacing the holes in the old instruments, making it more convenient to play. Named after the 19th-century German inventor Theobald Boehm.

Bogen (Ger., boh′gen). 1. A bow.—2. A slur, or a tie.

Bois (Fr., bwăh). "Wood"—the woodwinds.

Bolero (Sp., bŏh-leh′rŏh). 1. A Spanish dance in $\frac{3}{4}$ time and lively tempo (allegretto), the dancers accompanying their steps with castanets.—2. A composition in bolero style.

Bombard. A large kind of oboe or shawm, now obsolete.

Bongos. Paired, hand-held Cuban drums, struck by the fingertips.

Boogie-woogie. Type of jazz with ostinato bass figures.

Bop. Shortened name for Bebop.

Bossa nova. Popular Brazilian dance music influenced by American jazz.

Bouche (Fr., boosh). Mouth. . . *À bouche fermée*, same as *Bocca chiusa*.

Bouffe (Fr., boof). Comic, burlesque. . . *Opéra bouffe*, comic opera.

Bourdon (Fr., boor-dŏhn′). 1. An organ stop.—2. A great bell, as the bourdon of Notre-Dame.—3. The lowest string of the 'cello and double bass.

Bourrée (Fr., boo-rā′). 1. A dance of French or Spanish origin, in rapid tempo, having 2 sections of 8 measures each, and in $\frac{2}{4}$ or $\frac{4}{4}$ time.—2. A movement in Baroque suites, in *alla breve* time.

Boutade (Fr., boo-tăhd′). 1. A short impromptu ballet.—2. An instrumental impromptu or fantasia.

B

Bow. The implement used in playing instruments of the violin type. The *hair* is attached to the *stick* by a bent *point* or *head*, and drawn into proper tension by the sliding *nut*, which is worked by the *screw*. . . Bow-arm or -hand, the right arm or hand.

Bowing. The art of handling the bow; a player's method or style; also, the signs for, and manner of, executing any given passage.

Braccio (It., brah´cho). "Arm"; instruments held in the arms were designated *da braccio*, "of the arm."

Brace. 1. The character { which connects two or more staves indicating that the parts on these staves are to be played simultaneously.— 2. The group of staves so connected, as the *upper brace*.

Branle (Fr., brahn´l´). A 16th-century French dance in ¼ time, in which several persons joined hands and took the lead in turn.

Brass band. Differs from full military band by omission of reed instruments.

Bratsche (Ger., brah´chĕ). The viola.

Brautlied (Ger., browt´-lēt). Bridal or wedding song.

Bravo. A shout of acclaim for the performer, commonly used to hail an opera singer. The feminine form is *brava*.

Bravura (It., brăh-voo´răh). Boldness, dash, brilliancy. . . Aria di bravura, a vocal solo consisting of difficult passages, designed to show off the singer's skill.

Break. 1. The point where one register of a voice or instrument passes over into another; in the voice, the junction of the head and chest registers; in the clarinet, between the notes 2. An imperfect tone produced by incorrect lipping of a horn or trumpet; or by some difficulty with the reed of the clarinet (this "break" is called "the goose"); or, in singing, by some defect in the vocal chords.

Breath mark. A sign inserted in a vocal part to show that the singer may (or must) take breath at that point; written variously (', *, ✔, \/, ").

Breit (Ger., brīt). Broadly.

Breve (brēv). A note equal to 2 whole notes or semibreves; the longest used in modern notation; written:

Bridge. In bowed instruments, a thin, arching piece of wood set upright on the belly to raise and stretch the strings above the resonance box, to which the bridge communicates the vibrations of the strings.—In the piano, and other string instruments, a rail of wood or steel over which the strings are stretched.

Brillante (It., brēl-lăhn´tĕh). Brilliant, showy, sparkling.

Brindisi (It., brēn-dē´-zē). A drinking song.

Brio, con (It., kŏhn brē´ŏh). With gusto; spiritedly.

Brisé (Fr., brē-zā´; "broken"). In violin playing, short, detached strokes of the bow.

Broken cadence. See CADENCE. . . *Broken chords*, chords whose tones are sounded in succession instead of together (see ARPEGGIO). *Broken octaves*, series of octaves in which the higher tones alternate with the lower.

Brummstimmen (Ger., brŏŏm´shtim´men). "Humming voices," production of the tone without words, through the nose, with closed mouth (BOCCA CHIUSA).

Bruscamente (It., brŏŏ-skäh-men´tĕh). Brusquely or forcibly accented.

Buffo, -a (It., bŏŏf´fŏh,-fäh). Comic, burlesque; hence, *Buffo*, a comic actor in an opera. . . *Aria buffa*, a comic aria. . . *Opera buffa*, comic or burlesque opera.

Bugle. 1. A wind instrument of brass or copper, with cupped mouthpiece, used for infantry calls and signals.—2. The keyed bugle, with 6 keys, and a compass of over 2 octaves.—3. The valve bugle. See SAXHORN.

Bühne (Ger., bü´-ne). Stage.

Bühnenfestspiel (Ger., bü´nen-fĕst-spēl). Stage festival play.

Bühnenmusik (Ger., bü´-nen-moo-zĭk). Incidental music for plays or music performed on the stage.

Burden. 1. A chorus or refrain repeated after each stanza of a song.—2. The drone of a bagpipe.—3.The bass part.—4. A dance accompaniment sung without instruments.

Burlesco, -a (It., bŏŏr-lĕ´skŏh, -skäh). Comic, farcical.

Burlesque (bur-lesk´). A dramatic extravaganza, or farcical travesty of some serious subject, with more or less music.

C

C. 1. (Ger., *C*; Fr. *ut*; It. *do*). The first tone and degree in the typical diatonic scale of C major.—2. In music theory capital *C* designates the *C*-major triad, small *c* the *c*-minor triad.—3. Middle *C* is the note *c*¹ on the piano keyboard.

Cabaletta (It., käh-bäh-let′tah). In Italian opera, the concluding section of an aria, forming a summary in rapid tempo.

Caccia (It., cäht′chäh). The chase; a hunt. . . *Alla caccia*, in hunting style, that is, accompanied by horns.

Cacophony. A raucous conglomeration of sound.

Cadence. 1. A CADENZA.—2. Rhythm.—3. The closing strains of a melody or harmonized movement; the Close or ending of a phrase, section, or movement. . . *Amen cadence*, a popular term for *Plagal cadence* (to which the word "Amen" is often sung). . . *Authentic c.*, a cadence in which the penultimate chord is the dominant, and the final chord is the tonic. . . *Avoided, Broken, Deceptive, Evaded,* or *False c.*, a cadence that settles on an unexpected chord. . . *Full c.*, a Perfect cadence. . .*Half* or *Imperfect c.*, a cadence on any chord other than the tonic. . .*Interrupted* or *Irregular c.*, an unexpected progression avoiding some regular cadence. . . *Perfect c.*, an authentic cadence in which both dominant and tonic chords are in root position, and the last chord has the root in the highest voice as well as the tonic chord; the "authentic cadence" of the church modes. . . *Plagal c.*, the subdominant chord followed by the tonic. Many categories overlap.

Cadenza (It., käh-den′dzäh). 1. In a vocal solo, a brilliant passage, usually at the end.—2. An elaborate passage or fantasia at the end of the first or last movement of a concerto, and played by the solo instrument.

Caesura. The dividing line between two melodic and rhythmical phrases, often marked by a BREATH MARK.

Caisse (Fr., käss). Drum.

Caisse claire (Fr., käss klâr). Snare drum.

Caisse, grosse (Fr., grōs käss). Bass drum.

Caisse roulante (Fr., käss roo-lähn′t). Side drum.

Cakewalk. An American popular dance in ragtime rhythm.

Calliope (cal-li´o-pē). A steam organ; a pipe organ whose tone is produced by steam, instead of wind, under pressure.

Calmando(si) (It., kăhl-măhn´dŏh[-sē]). Growing calm, becoming tranquil.

Caloroso (It., kăh-lŏh-roh´sŏh). With warmth, passion; passionately.

Calypso. Popular music of the West Indies, with lyrics often reflecting topical subjects.

Cambiata (It., kăhm-byăh´tah). "Changed"; *nota cambiata*, a CHANGING NOTE.

Camera (It., kah´měh-răh). Chamber, room, small hall. . . *Alla camera*, in the style of chamber music. . . *Musica da camera*, chamber music.

Campana (It., kăhm-pah´năh). A bell.

Cancan. A fast French vaudeville dance in $\frac{2}{4}$ time, once regarded as naughty.

Canción (Sp., kăhn´thē-ŏn). Song.

Canon. The strictest form of musical imitation, in which 2 or more parts take up, in succession, the given subject note for note.

Canonical Hours. Established times for daily prayer in the Catholic Church: *matins* (including *nocturns* and *lauds*), *prime, terce, sext, nones, vespers,* and *compline*.

Canonic imitation. Strict imitation of one part by another.

Cantabile (It., kăhn-tah´bē-lěh). "Singable"; in a singing or vocal style.

Cantante (It., kăhn-tăhn´teh). Singing; smooth and flowing.

Cantata (It., kăhn-tah´tăh). A vocal work with instrumental accompaniment, consisting of choruses and solos, recitative, duets, etc., shorter than an oratorio. Cantatas may be *sacred* or *secular*.

Canticle. One of the nonmetrical hymns of praise and jubiliation in the Bible; or a sacred chant similar to it.

Cantilena (It., kăhn-tē-lâ´năh). "A little song"; a ballad or light popular song; a flowing, songlike passage on an instrument.

Cantillation. Chanting in a simple manner without accompaniment; usually applied to Jewish liturgy.

Canto (It., kăhn´tŏh). A melody, song, chant; the soprano (highest vocal or instrumental part). . . *Col canto,* "with the melody," a direction to accompanists to follow the solo part in tempo and expression. . . *Canto fermo,* a Cantus firmus.

Cantor. The leading singer in German Protestant church services or in Jewish synagogues.

Cantus firmus (Latin). A fixed or given melody: (*a*) Plainsong; (*b*) in counterpoint, a given melody, to which other parts are to be set according to rule.

Canzone (It., kăhn-tsoh´nĕh). A song, folk song; also, a part-song in madrigal style.

Canzonet. A little air or song; a short part-song; a madrigal.

Capriccio (It., kăh-prit´chŏh). An instrumental piece of free form, distinguished by originality in harmony and rhythm; a Caprice . . . *A capriccio*, at pleasure.

Capriccioso (It., kăh-prit-chŏh´sŏh). In a capricious, fanciful, fantastic style.

Carezzevole (It., kăh-ret-sā´vŏh-lĕh). Caressingly, soothingly.

Carillon (Fr., kăh-rē-yöhn´). 1. A Glockenspiel, or set of fixed bells played from a keyboard or by a barrel mechanism.

Carol. To sing joyously; hence, a joyous Christmas song of praise.

Cassa (It., kăh´săh). Drum.

Cassa, gran (It., grähn´ kăh´săh). Bass drum.

Cassation. 18th-century instrumental suite, similar to the *Divertimento* and *Serenade*.

Castanets. A pair of small concave pieces of wood or ivory, attached by a cord to a dancer's thumb and forefinger, and struck together in time with the music.

Castrato (It., kăh-strah´tŏh). An adult male singer with soprano or alto voice.

Catch. A round or canon for 3 or more voices. Catches are usually humorous.

Cavatina (It., kăh-văh-tē´năh). A song; particularly, a short aria without second section or *Da capo*.

C clef. A clef written 𝄡

C dur. (Ger., tsā door´). *C* major.

Cédez (Fr., sā-dā´). Go slower.

Celesta. Percussion instrument invented by Mustel in Paris, 1888, consisting of tuned steel bars connected to a keyboard.

'Cello (It., chel´lŏh). Abbreviation of VIOLONCELLO.

Cembalo (It., chĕm´băh-lŏh). Harpsichord, piano. . . *A cembalo*, for keyboard.

Ces (Ger., tsĕss). *C* flat.

Ces dur (Ger., tsĕss door). *C* flat major.

Ceses (Ger., tsĕss´ĕss). *C* double flat.

Cha-cha. Latin American dance in binary rhythm; sometimes called Cha-cha-cha.

Chaconne (Fr., shäh-kohn´). An instrumental piece consisting of a series of variations above a ground bass not over 8 measures in length, in $\frac{3}{4}$ time and slow tempo.

Chalumeau (Fr., shäh-lü-moh´). An old wind instrument having 9 finger holes and a beating reed. See CLARINET.

Chamber music. Vocal or instrumental music suitable for performance in a room or small hall; especially, quartets and similar concerted pieces for solo instruments.

Chamber opera. An opera suitable for performance in a small hall, with a limited number of performers and accompanied by a chamber orchestra.

Chamber orchestra. A small orchestra.

Chamber symphony. A symphony for chamber orchestra.

Chance music. See ALEATORY.

Change. 1. In harmony, MODULATION.—2. In the voice, MUTATION.

Change-ringing. The art of ringing a peal of bells in varying and systematic order.

Changing note. A dissonant note entering on the strong beat, and passing by a step to a consonance, or by a skip to a chord note or a note belonging to another chord.

Chanson (Fr., shähn-sŏhn´). A song.

Chant. A short sacred song.—1. Gregorian chant is a Gregorian melody repeated with several verses of biblical prose text; it has 5 divisions, (1) the intonation, (2) the first dominant, or reciting-note, (3) the mediation, (4) the 2nd dominant, or reciting-note, and (5) the cadence.—2. See ANGLICAN CHANT.

Chant (Fr., shähn). Song; singing; melody; tune. Also, voice (the vocal part as distinguished from the accompaniment).

Chanter. The melody-pipe of the bagpipe.

Chanterelle (Fr., shähn-t´-rel´). The highest string on a violin, lute, etc.

Chanty. See SHANTY.

Chapel. A company of musicians attached to the establishment of any distinguished personage.

Character piece. A piece depicting a definite mood, impression, scene, or event.

Characteristic tone. 1. The leading tone.—2. That tone in any key which specially distinguishes it from nearly related keys; like $F\sharp$ in G major, distinguishing it from C major.

Chef d'orchestre (Fr., shef dor-kes´tr). Conductor of an orchestra.

Chest of viols. Old English description of a set of string instruments of various sizes, kept in a specially constructed chest.

Chest register. The lower register of the male or female voice, the tones of which produce sympathetic vibration in the chest.

Chest tone, chest voice. Vocal tone possessing the quality of the chest register.

Chiaramente (It., k'yăh-răh-men´tĕh). Clearly, distinctly, limpidly.

Chiesa (It., kee-eh´sah). Church; used in definitions such as *sonata da chiesa*, a sonata suitable for church performance.

Chime. 1. A set of from 5 to 12 bells tuned to the scale, and played by swinging either the bells themselves or clappers hung within them. Also, a tune so played.—2. A set of bells and hammers played by a keyboard; a Carillon.

Chinese blocks. Resonant wood blocks struck with a drumstick or mallet.

Chin rest. An oval plate of ebony attached to the edge of the violin to the left of the tailpiece.

Chitarra (It., kē-tar´răh). A guitar.

Chitarrone (It., kee-tar-roh´neh). A large lute.

Chiuso, -a (It., kew´sŏh, -săh). Closed. . . *A bocca chiusa*, with closed mouth; humming.

Choeur (Fr., kühr). Chorus.

Choir. 1. A company of singers, especially in a church.—2. A choral society.—3. A subdivision of a chorus; for example, the 1st and 2nd choirs in 8-part music.

Choirmaster. Leader (leading singer) of a choir.

Choral. Relating or pertaining to a chorus, or to vocal concerted music.

Chorale (kŏh-rahl´). A hymn tune of the German Protestant Church, or one similar in style.

Chorale prelude. An instrumental composition based on a chorale or hymn tune.

Chord. 1. A harmony of 3 or more tones.—2. A *flat* or *solid* chord is one whose tones are produced simultaneously, opposed to *broken*.—3. A string.

Choreography. The dancing scenario in a ballet.

Chôros. A Brazilian folk dance, or a work written in a Brazilian folk style.

Chorus. A company of singers; hence, a composition, most often in 4 parts, each sung by several or many singers; a double chorus has 8 parts. Also, the refrain or burden of a song.

Christe eleison (Gk., crēs´tā ā-lā´ā-sohn, "Christ, have mercy"). Part of the Kyrie.

Chromatic. Tones foreign to a given key or chord; opposed to diatonic. *Chromatic signs*, the sharp (♯), flat (♭), natural (♮), double sharp (𝄪), and double flat (♭♭).

Church modes. The octave scales employed in medieval church music.

Ciaccona (It., chăhk-koh´năh). A CHACONNE.

Cimbalo (It., chĭm´băh-lŏh). A cymbal; a harpsichord; a tambourine.

Cimbalom. A large dulcimer, typical of Hungarian Gypsy bands.

Cinelli (It., chĭn-nĕl´lē). Cymbals.

Circle of Fifths. A series of fifths tuned in equal temperament, so that the *twelfth* fifth in the series has the same letter name as the first tone.

Circular canon. A canon closing in the key a semitone above that in which it begins; 12 repetitions would thus carry it through the "circle" of 12 keys.

Cis (Ger., tsiss). *C* sharp.

Cis dur (Ger., tsiss door). In German, *C* sharp major.

Cis moll (Ger., tsiss mohl). *C* sharp minor.

Cisis (Ger., tsiss´iss). *C* double sharp.

Cither (sith´er), **Cithern, Cittern** (sit´-ern). A kind of lute or guitar, strung with wire and played with a pick; used in the 16th and 17th centuries.

Claque. Hired groups of people paid to applaud an opera singer or other performer.

Clarinet. A transposing wind instrument derived from the Chalumeau. It has a cylindrical wooden or metal tube pierced by 18 holes, 13 being closed by keys, yielding a chromatic series of 19 prime tones (*e* to *b* ¹♭). Its compass comprises 3 octaves in 4 different registers; the Low register ("chalumeau"), Medium register, High register ("clarinetto"), and Super-acute register.

Clarion. A small, shrill-toned trumpet.

Classical music. 1. European music from about 1770 to 1830.—2. Colloquially, any serious music, as opposed to popular music.

Classical suite. An instrumental suite of dance forms, also called the *Baroque Suite*. It has 4 principal movements; Allemande, Courante, Sarabande, and Gigue. Lighter dance movements, such as the Minuet, Bourrée, and Gavotte, are often interpolated between the Sarabande and the Gigue.

Clavecin (Fr., klăh-v´-săn´), **Clavicembalo** (It., klăh-vē-chem´băh-lŏh). Harpsichord.

Claves. Hardwood sticks used in Latin American rhythm bands, which produce a sharp sound when clicked together.

Clavichord. A precursor of the piano, differing in its action in having, instead of hammers, upright metal wedges called tangents on the rear end of the keys; on pressing a key, the tangent strikes the wire and remains pressed against it until the finger is lifted, causing only one section of the string to vibrate.

Clavier (klä-vēr′). A keyboard. See KLAVIER.

Clef. A character set at the head of the staff to fix the pitch or position of one note, and thus of the rest.

Cloches (Fr., klōsh). Chimes.

Close (klōz). A cadence ending a section, movement, or piece.

Close harmony. In regular 4-voice settings, the 3 upper voices are placed within an octave in close harmony.

C moll (Ger., tsä mohl). *C* minor.

Coda (It., koh′däh). A "tail"; hence, a passage ending a movement.

Codetta (It., kŏh-det′täh). A short coda.

Color. 1. Timbre.—2. In 14th- and 15th-century isorhythmic music, a repeated pitch pattern.

Coloratura (It., kŏh-lŏh-răh-too′răh). Vocal runs, passages, trills, etc., enhancing the brilliancy of a composition and displaying the singer's skill.

Combo. A jazz ensemble; the word is short for combination.

Come prima (It., kô′mĕh prē′mäh). As before, as at first (that is, "resume the previous tempo").

Come sopra (It., kô′mĕh soh′präh). As above.

Come sta (It., kô′mĕh stah). As it stands, as written.

Comic opera. 1. Opera with a comic subject.—2. See OPÉRA COMIQUE.

Comma. The Greek term for the minute interval that represents the difference between a perfect fifth in tempered pitch and the pure interval formed in the natural harmonic series.

Common chord. A major or minor triad.

Common time. A measure containing 2 (or 4) half notes, or 4 quarter notes, with 2 or 4 beats respectively; duple or quadruple time.

Comodo (It., kô′mŏh-dŏh). Easy, leisurely, at a convenient pace.

Compass. The range of a voice or instrument; the scale of all the tones it can produce, from the lowest to the highest.

Complement, Complementary interval. An interval which, added to any given interval not wider than an octave, completes the octave; a fourth is the complement of a fifth, a minor third of a major sixth, etc.

Compline. A short evening service, completing the 7 Canonical Hours.

Composition. The broadest term for writing music in any form.

Compound meter. A measure with a number of beats composed of 2 or more different simple meters such as 5/4 (2/4 + 3/4) or 7/4 (4/4 + 3/4).

Con (It., kŏhn). With; in a style expressive of. For definitions of phrases beginning with "con," see the second word in the given phrase.

Concert. A musical performance requiring the cooperation of several musicians.

Concertante (It., kŏhn-châr-tähn´tĕh). 1. A concert piece.—2. A composition for 2 or more solo voices or instruments with accompaniment by orchestra or organ, in which each solo part is in turn brought into prominence.—3. A composition for 2 or more unaccompanied solo instruments in orchestral music. . . *Concertante style*, a style admitting of a brilliant display of skill on the soloist's part.

Concertina. The improved accordion invented by Wheatstone in 1829.

Concert grand. A grand piano.

Concertino. 1. A small concerto, scored for a small ensemble.—2. The group of soloists in a CONCERTO GROSSO.

Concertmaster. The leader of the first violin section in the orchestra.

Concerto (It., kŏhn-chăr´tŏh). An extended composition for a solo instrument, usually with orchestral accompaniment, and in (modified) sonata form.

Concerto grosso (It., kŏhn-châr´tŏh´ grô´sŏh). An instrumental composition employing a small group of solo instruments against a larger group or full orchestra. See CONCERTINO.

Concerto for orchestra. A symphonic work in which the orchestral instruments play the role of soloists.

Concert overture. An overture for full orchestra, performed as an independent composition at a symphony concert.

Concert pitch. The actual sound produced by an instrument, as distinct from a written note in transposing instruments. Thus in the *B* flat clarinet, the written note *C* sounds *B* flat, which is the concert pitch.

Concertstück (Ger., kŏhn-tsârt´shtük). Concert piece; concerto.

Concitato (It., kŏhn-chē-tah´tŏh). Moved, excited, agitated.

Concrete music. See MUSIQUE CONCRÉTE.

Conduct. The "leading" of a part.

Conductor. Director of an orchestra or chorus.

Conductus. A contrapuntal part combined with a given original melody in polyphonic music of the Middle Ages.

Conical mouthpiece. See CUPPED. . . *Conical tube*, one tapering very gradually; a *cylindrical tube* does not taper.

Consequent. In a canon, the Follower; the part imitating the antecedent or Leader.

Console. The organ's keyboard, stops, and pedals.

Consonance. A combination of two or more tones, harmonious and pleasing in itself, and requiring no further progression to make it satisfactory. . . *Imperfect consonances*, the major and minor Thirds and Sixths. . . *Perfect consonances*, the Octave, Fifth, and Fourth.

Consort. An old English term for an instrumental ensemble; a *whole consort* consisted of all wind or all string instruments while a *broken consort* was a mixed group.

Contra (L.; It). "Against"; prefixed to instrument names, it means "octave below."

Contrabass. A double bass.

Contradanza (It., kŏhn-trăh-dahn´tzăh). Italian name for the English COUNTRY DANCE.

Contrafagotto (It., kŏhn-trăhf-făh-gŏht´tŏh). Double bassoon.

Contralto (It., kăhn-trăhl´tăh). See ALTO 1.

Contra-octave. The octave below the GREAT OCTAVE.

Contrary motion. Parts progress in contrary motion when one moves up while the other moves down.

Contre (Fr., kăhn´tr). "Against"; contra-, counter-.

Contredanse (Fr., kăhn-truh-dahns´). French name for the English COUNTRY DANCE.

Cool. An American JAZZ style of the 1950s, characterized by a less frenetic ("hot") atmosphere than earlier styles, use of "nonjazz" instruments (flute, French horn), and adoption of "classical" techniques (fugue).

Coperto (It., kăh-pâr´tăh). Covered, muffled.

Cor (Fr., kor). A horn. . . *Cor anglais* (ăhn-glä´), the English horn.

Corda (It., kôr´dăh). A string. . . *Sopra una corda*, play "on one string" . . . *Una corda*, use soft pedal of piano. . . *Due corde*, release soft pedal, or play with soft pedal pressed halfway down. . . In violin playing, "play the note on two strings". . . *Tutte (le) corde*, "all the strings"; that, is "release the soft pedal". . . *Corda vuota*, open string.

Cornemuse. French word for bagpipe.

Cornet. A brass instrument of the trumpet family, with conical tube and cupped mouthpiece; improved from the post-horn by the addition of 3 valves; medium compass 2 octaves and 3 tones; it is a transposing instrument in Bb.—The old cornet was a wooden instrument with finger holes.

Cornet à pistons (Fr., kôr-nā´ ăh pēs-tŏhn´). The ordinary valve cornet.

Corno (It., kôr-nōh). A horn (plural *corni*).

Corrente (It., kŏhr-ren´těh). Courante.

Cotillion (Fr., *cotillon* [kŏh-tē-yŏhn´]). A French or German dance to quadrille music.

Coulé (Fr., koo-lā´). *Legato*, slurred; also, a harpsichord GRACE NOTE.

Counter. Any part set to contrast with the principal part or melody; specifically, the *countertenor* (high tenor, or alto). . . *Bass counter*, a second bass part. . . *Counterexposition*, reentrance of a fugue subject. . .*Countersubject*, a fugal theme following the subject in the same part. . . *Countertenor*, a voice usually developed from the headtones and falsetto of a bass voice; compass from *g* to *c* ^{2}.

Counterpoint. 1. The art of polyphonic composition.—2. Composition with 2 or more simultaneous melodies. . . *Double Counterpoint* is written so that the upper part can become the lower part, and vice versa. . .In *triple* and *quadruple counterpoint*, 3 and 4 parts are written so that they can be mutually exchanged.

Country dance. A dance in $\frac{2}{4}$ or $\frac{3}{4}$ time, in which the partners form two opposing lines which advance and retreat, the couples also dancing down the lines and returning to their places.

Country/Western. A term covering a variety of American rural and cowboy styles.

Couplet. 1. Two successive lines forming a pair, usually rhymed.—2. In triple times, 2 equal notes occupying the time of 3 such notes in the regular rhythm.

Courante (Fr., koo-răhn´t). An old French dance in $\frac{3}{2}$ time.

Covered. See OCTAVE. . . *Covered strings*, strings of silk, wire, or gut, covered with spiral turns of fine silver or copper wire.

Crab canon. A canon performed backwards.

Credo (L., crā´doh). "I believe"; part of the Mass.

Crescendo (It., krěh-shen´dŏh). Swelling, increasing in loudness.

Crescent; also **Chinese crescent,** or **Pavilion.** An instrument of Turkish origin used in military music; it has crescent-shaped brass plates hung around a staff and topped by a cap or pavilion; around the plates little bells are hung, which are jingled in time with the music.

Croche (Fr., krohsh). An eighth note.

Crook. A short tube, bent or straight, which can be fitted to the main tube of a horn or trumpet to lower the pitch.

Cross relation. Same as FALSE RELATION.

Crotchet. A quarter note. . . *Crotchet-rest*, a quarter rest.

Crucifixus (L., kroo-chē-fĕx´oos). Part of the Mass, in the Credo section.

Crwth (krŭth). An ancient Celtic bowed instrument, probably the oldest European instrument of its class. Its square body was terminated by 2 parallel arms joined at the end by a crossbar, the center of which supported the fingerboard; it had originally 3, in modern times 6, strings. Also spelled *Crouth* or *Crowd.*

Csárdás (Hungarian, char′dahsh). A national Hungarian dance, distinguished by its passionate character and changing tempos.

Cue. A phrase occurring near the end of a long pause in another part, and inserted in small notes *in the latter* to serve as a guide in timing its reentrance.

Cuivré (Fr., kyuh-eev-ray′). With a brassy tone, as played particularly on the horn.

Cupped mouthpiece. The shallower, cup-shaped form of mouthpiece for brass wind instruments; the *conical* (cone-shaped) mouthpiece is the deeper form.

Cut time. See ALLA BREVE.

Cymbals. 1. The orchestral cymbals are 2 concave plates of brass or bronze, with broad, flat rims, and holes for the straps by which they are held.—2. See ANTIQUE CYMBAL.

D

D

D (Ger., *D*; Fr. *ré*; It., *re*). The 2nd tone and degree in the typical diatonic scale of *C* major.—In music theory, capital *D* designates the *D*-major triad, small *d* the *d*- minor triad.—*D.* also stands for *Da* (D.C. = *Da capo*) and *Dal* (D.S. = *Dal segno*).

Da (It., dah). By, from, for, of. . . *Da capo*, from the beginning. . . *Da capo al fine*, repeat from beginning to the word *Fine*, or to a hold. . . *Da capo al segno*, from the beginning the sign (𝄋). . . *D.C. al segno, poi (segue) la coda*, from the beginning to the sign, then play the coda. . .*D.C. dal segno*, repeat from the sign.

Dactyl(e) (L., *dactylus*, a finger). A metrical foot with syllables arranged like the fingerjoints, one long and two short; the accent on the first: – ◡ ◡.

Dagli (dăhl´yē). **dai** (dah´ē), **dal, dall', dalla, dalle, dallo** (It.). To the, by the, for the, from the, etc.

Dal segno (It., dăhl sān´yōh). From the sign. . . *Dal segno al fine*, from the sign to the end.

Damper. 1. A mechanical device for checking the vibration of the piano string. . . *Damper pedal*, the right, or loud, pedal.—2. The *mute* of a brass instrument.

Danza. Italian and Spanish word for *dance.*

D dur (Ger., dā door). *D* major.

Deceptive cadence. A cadence leading to the chord of the sixth degree of the scale instead of the expected tonic chord. Sometimes called *interrupted cadence.*

Decibel. A scientific unit for the measurement of loudness or intensity of sound.

Declamando (It., dā-klăh-măhn´dŏh). "Declaiming"; in declamatory style.

Declamation. In vocal music, clear and correct enunciation of the words.

Decrescendo (It., dā-crĕh-shen´dŏh). Decreasing in loudness.

Degli (It., dāl´yē). Of the; than the.

Degree. 1. One of the 8 consecutive tones in a major or minor diatonic scale. Degrees are counted upward from the keynote.—2. A line or space on the staff.—3. A step.

Dehors, en (Fr., än dĕ-or). "Outside"—with emphasis.

Dei (dā´ē), **Del, dell' della, delle, dello** (It.). Of the, than the.

Delayed resolution. See Resolution.

Delicatezza, con (It., kŏhn dĕh-lē-kah-tet´săh). With delicacy.

Demiquaver. A sixteenth note.

Demisemiquaver. A thirty-second note.

Depress. To lower (as by a ♭ or ♭♭). . . *Depression*, chromatic lowering of a tone.

Derivative. 1. The inversion of a fundamental chord.—2. The root of a chord.

Des (Ger., dess). *D* flat.

Descant. Same as DISCANT.

Des dur (Ger., dess door). *D* flat major.

Deses (Ger., dess´ess). *D* double flat.

Destra (It., dĕh´sträh). Right. . . *Mano destra (destra mano, colla destra)*, "play with the right hand." (Abbreviated *m. d.*)

Détaché (Fr., dā-tăh-shā´). In violin playing, "detached," that is, playing successive notes with downbow and upbow in alteration, but not staccato. . . *Grand détaché*, a whole stroke of the bow to each note.

Deux (Fr., dö). Two. . . *À deux mains*, for 2 hands. . . *Deux temps*, or *Valse à deux temps*, a "two-step" waltz.

Development. The working out or evolution (elaboration) of a theme by presenting it in varied melodic, harmonic, or rhythmic treatment.

Di (It., dē). Of, from, to, by; than.

Diapason. 1. An octave.—2. Either of the 2 principal foundation stops of the organ, both of 8´ pitch. *Pedal* diapasons are usually 16´ stops.—3. Compass of a voice or instrument.—4. A fixed pitch; "normal diapason" is an accepted standard of pitch.

Diaphony. Literally, "sounding through"; a form of medieval counterpoint allowing certain liberties in crossing of parts and in using passing dissonances.

Diatonic. By, through, with, within, or embracing the tones of the standard major or minor scale. . . *Diatonic harmony* or *melody*, that employing the tones of only one scale. . . *Diatonic instrument*, one yielding only the tones of that scale of which its fundamental tone is the keynote. . . *Diatonic interval*, one formed by 2 tones of the same scale. . . *Diatonic modulation*, see MODULATION. . . *Diatonic progression*, stepwise progression within one scale. . . *Diatonic scale*, see SCALE.

Diesis (It., dē-ā-sĭs). Sharp; the sign ♯.

Differential tone. A tone produced by the difference of the frequencies of vibration between 2 notes when played loudly on a string instrument; such a tone lies well beneath the original 2 sounds, and produces a jarring effect; sometimes it is called "wolf tone."

Diminished interval. A perfect or minor interval contracted by a chromatic semitone. . . *Diminished chord*, one whose highest and lowest tones form a diminished interval. . . *Diminished triad*, a root with minor Third and diminished Fifth.

Diminished seventh chord. A chord consisting of 3 conjunct minor thirds, forming the interval of the diminished seventh between the top and bottom notes.

Diminution. The repetition or imitation of a theme in notes of smaller time value.

Di molto (It. dē mŏhl'tŏh). Very, extremely; *allegro di molto*, extremely fast.

Direct. The sign ⌒⌄ or ⌄ set at the end of a staff to show the position of the first note on the next staff.

Dirge. A funeral hymn or composition written to commemorate the dead.

Dis (Ger., dĭs). *D* sharp.

Discant. 1. The first attempts at polyphony with contrary motion in the parts (12th century); opposed to the *organum*, in which parallel motion was the rule.—2. Treble or soprano voice; the highest part in part music.

Disinvoltura, con (It., kŏhn dē-zin-vŏhl-too'rah). With ease, grace; flowingly.

Disis (Ger., dĭs'ĭs). *D* double sharp.

Disjunct motion. Progression by leaps.

Dis moll (Ger., dĭs mohl). *D* sharp minor.

Dissonance. A combination of 2 or more tones requiring resolution.

Dissonant interval. Two tones forming a dissonance. The dissonant intervals are the seconds, sevenths, and all diminished and augmented intervals. . . *Dissonant chord*, one containing one or more dissonant intervals.

Divertimento (It., dē-vâr-tē-men'tŏh), **Divertisssement** (Fr., dē-vâr-tĕs-mähn'). A light and easy piece of instrumental music. Also, an instrumental composition in 6 or 7 movements, like a serenade. Also, an *entr'acte* in an opera, in the form of a short ballet, etc.

Divisi (It. dē-vē'zē). "Divided." Signifies that 2 parts written on one staff are not to be played as double stops, but by the division into 2 bodies of the instruments playing from that staff.

Division. A "dividing up" of a melodic series of tones into a rapid coloratura passage; if for voice, the passage was to be sung in one breath.—*To run a division*, to execute such a passage. . . *Division-viol*, the Viola da gamba.

Dixieland. An American JAZZ style which became prominent in the 1920s. It is ensemble music—the instruments are typically trumpet (or cornet), clarinet, piano, banjo, and drums—and is characterized by collective improvisation, dotted rhythms, and syncopation.

D moll (Ger., deh mohl). *D* minor.

Do (It., doh). 1. The note *C*.—2. In solmization, the usual syllable name for the 1st degree of the scale. In the *fixed Do* method of teaching, Do is the name for all notes bearing the letter-name *C*, whether keynotes or not; in the *movable Do* method, Do is always the keynote.

Dodecaphony. Technique of composition developed by Schoenberg and others about 1925, in which the basic theme of a given composition contains 12 different notes; the name is derived from the Greek words *dodeca*, "twelve," and *phone*, "sound." In dodecaphonic writing the key signature is abolished and the concept of tonality undergoes a radical change; furthermore, dissonances are emancipated and are used on a par with consonant combinations.

Dolce (It., döhl'chĕh). 1. Sweet, soft, suave.—2. A sweet-toned organ stop.

Dolcian (Ger., döhl-tsiahn'). 1. An early kind of bassoon—2. An organ stop.

Dolente (It., döh-len'tĕh). Doleful, plaintive, sad.

Doloroso (It., döh-löh-roh'söh). In a style expressive of pain or grief.

Dominant. The fifth tone in the major or minor scale. . . *Dom. chord,* *(a)* the dominant triad; *(b)* the dom. chord of the 7th. . . *Dom. section* of a movement, a section written in the key of the dominant, lying between and contrasting with 2 others in the key of the tonic. . . *Dom. triad,* that having the dominant as root.

Domra. A Russian balalaika.

Doppel (Ger., döhp'pĕl). Double.

Doppelgriff (Ger., döhp'pel-grēf). Double stop (violin); *Doppelgriffe,* Thirds, Sixths, etc., played with one hand (piano).

Doppelkreuz (Ger., döhp'pel-kroytz). Double sharp.

Doppio (It., dô'pĭ-öh). Double. . . *Doppio movimento,* twice as fast . . . *Doppio note* or *doppio valore,* twice as slow (that is, the absolute time value of the notes is doubled). . . *Doppio pedale,* pedal part in octaves.

Dorian mode. A church mode corresponding to the scale from *D* to *D* as played on white keys of the piano.

Dot. A dot set after a note prolongs its time value by half; a second or third dot prolongs the time value of the dot immediately preceding it by half.

Double. 1. A variation.—2. To play or sing two different parts within the same piece.—3. "Producing a tone an octave lower"; as double bassoon, double bass, etc.—4. To add the higher or lower octave.

Double bar. The 2 vertical lines drawn through the staff at the end of a section, movement, or piece.

Double bass. The largest and deepest-toned instrument of the violin family.

D

Double chorus. One for 2 choirs, or divided choir, usually in 8 parts.

Double counterpoint. See COUNTERPOINT.

Double croche (Fr., doo-ble crosh'). A sixteenth note.

Double flat. The sign ♭♭

Double fugue. One with 2 themes.

Double octave. A 15th, or the interval of 2 octaves.

Double quartet. A quartet for 2 sets of 4 solo voices, or of 4 solo instruments.

Double reed. The reed used for instruments of the oboe family; 2 separate pieces of cane bound together to produce a characteristic vibration.

Double sharp. The sign ✕

Double stop. In violin playing, to stop 2 strings together, obtaining 2-part harmony.

Double tongue. In playing the flute and certain brass instruments, the application of the tongue in rapid alternation to the upper front teeth and the palate to obtain a clear-cut and brilliant staccato.

Douce (doos), **Doux** (doo) (Fr.). Soft, sweet, suave.

Downbeat. 1. The downward stroke of the hand in beating time, which marks the primary or first accent in each measure.—2. Hence, the accent itself.

Down-bow. In violin playing, the downward stroke of the bow from nut to point; on the 'cello and double bass, the stroke from nut to point. Usual sign ⊓

Doxology. A song of praise to God used in Roman Catholic and Protestant services. The word comes from Greek *Doxa*, "glory," and *Logos*, "saying."

Drame lyrique (Fr., drähm lē-rēk'). French designation for opera.

Dramma per musica (It., drähm-mäh pĕr moo'zē-käh). Literally, "drama by music"; a designation used at the birth of opera in Italy about 1600.

Drammatico (It., drähm-mäh'tē-koh). Dramatically; in a vivid, dramatic style.

Drängend (Ger., dreng'ent). Pressing, hastening; *stringendo.*

Drei (Ger., drī). Three.

Dreifach (Ger., drī'fäyh). Triple.

Drohend (Ger., drŏh'ent). Menacing.

Droit (Fr., drwäh). Right; *main droite,* right hand.

Drone. In the bagpipe, a continuously sounding pipe of constant pitch; a drone-pipe. . . *Drone-bass,* a bass on the tonic, or tonic and dominant, which is persistent throughout a movement or piece, as in the MUSETTE 2.

Drum. A percussion instrument consisting of a cylindrical, hollow *body* of wood or metal, over one or both ends of which a membrane (the *head*) is stretched tightly by means of a *hoop,* to which is attached an endless *cord* tightened by leather *braces,* or by rods and screws.

D string. The 3rd string on the violin; 2nd on the viola, 'cello, and double bass.

Due (It., doo´ĕh). Two. . . *A due, (a)* for 2; *(b)* both together (after *Divisi*). . . *Due corde,* see CORDA. . . *Due volte,* twice. . . *I due pedali,* both pedals at once.

Duet. A composition for 2 performers.

Dulciana. 1. An organ stop, having metal pipes of a somewhat sharp, thin tone.—2. A small reed stop of delicate tone.—3. A small bassoon.

Dulcimer. An ancient string instrument having wire strings stretched over a soundboard or resonance box, and struck with mallets or hammers.

Dumka (Polish, dŏŏm´kăh). A vocal or instrumental Romance of a melancholy cast.

Duo (It., doo´ŏh). A duet.—*Duo* is sometimes distinguished from *Duet* by applying the former term to a composition for 2 voices or instruments of *different* kinds, and the latter to a composition for 2 voices or instruments of the *same* kind.

Duple. Double. . . *Duple rhythm,* rhythm of 2 beats to a measure.

Dur (Ger., door). Major, as in *C dur* (C major), etc.

Durchführung (Ger., doorh´für-öŏng^k). "Through leading."—1. The development section in sonata form.—2. The exposition in a fugue.

Durchkomponiert (Ger., doorh-kom-poh-neert´). "Through-composed." A description of a song form in which every subsequent stanza has a different musical setting.

Duro, -a (It., doo´roh, -rah). Hard, harsh.

Düster (Ger., dü´ster). Gloomy, mournful.

Dux. The subject in a fugue; literally, "leader" in Latin.

Dynamics. The varying and contrasting degrees of loudness in musical tones.

E

E (Ger., *E*; Fr. and It. *mi*). The 3rd tone and degree in the typical diatonic scale of *C* major.

E (It.,ā). And.—When preceding a word beginning with "e," it should be written *ed*; before other vowels, either *e* or *ed* may be used; before consonants, only *e*.

Eccitato (It., ẹt-chē-tah′tŏh). Excited.

Ecclesiastical modes. The octave scales employed in medieval church music.

Echo. A subdued repetition of a strain or phrase.

Eco (It., ĕh′kŏh). Echo.

Écossaise (Fr., ā-kŏh-säz′). Originally, a Scotch round dance in ⅜ or ¾ time; now, a lively contredanse in ¾ time. Compare SCHOTTISCHE.

Ed (It., ed). And. See E.

Edel (Ger., ā′del). Noble; refined, chaste.

E dur (Ger., eh door). *E* major.

Eguaglianza, con (It., kŏhn ā-guăhl-yähn′tsäh). Evenly, smoothly.

Eguale (It., ā-guah′lĕh). Equal; even, smooth.

Eighteenth. Interval of 2 octaves and a fourth.

Eighth. 1. An octave.—2. An eighth note.

Eilend (Ger., ī′lent). Hastening; *stringendo.*

Ein, Eins (Ger., īn, īns). One.

Einfach (Ger., īn′făh). Simple; simply; *semplice.*

Eingang (Ger., īn′găhngᵏ). Introduction.

Einklang (Ger., īn′klăhngᵏ). Unison, consonance.

Einleitung (Ger., īn′lĭ-toongᵏ). Introduction.

Einsatz (Ger., īn′săhtz). 1. An attack.—2. An entrance of a part.

Einstimmig (Ger., īn′shtĭm-mĭyh). Monophonic, one-voiced.

Eis (Ger., ā′iss). *E* sharp.

Electric guitar. Electronically amplified guitar, widely used in rock groups.

Electronic music. Music that uses tones produced by electronic means. The earliest electronic instruments were the Theremin and the Ondes Martenot (1920s). Synthesizers, in use today, are capable of generating any desired pitch, scale, rhythm, tone color, or degree of loudness. They are often connected to computers through MIDI technology.

Electronic organ. An organ activated not by pipes but by electrical devices and capable of unlimited tone production.

Eleganza, con (It., kŏhn ā-lā-gähn′tsäh). In an elegant, graceful, refined style.

Elegy. A composition of a melancholy cast, having no fixed form.

Elevazione, con (It., kŏhn ā-lā-väh-tsē-oh′nĕh). In a lofty, elevated style.

Embellishment. See GRACE.

Embouchure (Fr., ähn-boo-shür′). The mouthpiece of a wind instrument; also the manipulation of the lips and tongue in playing a wind instrument.

E moll (Ger., eh mohl). *E* minor.

Empfindungsvoll (Ger., em-pfin′dŏŏngs-fŏhl). With emotion, feelingly, full of feeling.

Enchaînez (Fr., ähn-shä-nā′). "Go on directly"; *attaccate.*

Encore (Fr., ähn-kor′). "Again!" Used in English when recalling an actor or singer. —Also, a recall on the stage; or, the piece or performance repeated or added.

En élargissant (Fr., ähn ā-lar-zhē-sähn′). *Allargando.*

Energisch (Ger., ă-nâr′gish). With energy and decision, energetically.

Enfatico (It., en-fäh′tē-kŏh). With emphasis, emphatic.

English horn. An instrument of the oboe family, which transposes a fifth below the written note.

Enharmonic tones. Tones derived from different degrees, but practically identical in pitch, such as $C\sharp$ and $D\flat$... *Enharmonic chords* are chords differing in notation but alike in sound; such chords are called "enharmonically changed," and passing from one to the other is an "enharmonic modulation"... *Enharmonic interval,* one formed between 2 enharmonic tones.

Ensemble (Fr., ähn-sähn′bl′). 1. A group of performers who play together.—2. General effect or style of a performance...*Morceau d'ensemble,* concerted piece.

Entr'acte (Fr., ähn-trähkt′). "Interval between acts"; hence, a light instrumental composition or short ballet, for performance between acts.

Entrata (It., en-trah′täh), **Entrée** (Fr., ähn-trā′). 1. The orchestral prelude to a ballet, following the overture.—2. A division in a ballet like a "scene" in a play.—3. An old dance like a Polonaise, usually in $\frac{4}{4}$ time.

Entschlossen (Ger., ent-shlŏshs′sen). Resolutely, in a determined manner.

Episode (ep′ĭ-sōd). An intermediate or incidental section; in the fugue, a digression from the principal theme, interpolated between the developments of the latter.

Epithalamium. A wedding hymn.

Equabilmente (It., ā-kwăh-bēl-men′tĕh). Evenly, smoothly.

Equal temperament. See TEMPERAMENT.

Ergriffen (Ger., âr-grif′fen). Affected, stirred.

Erhaben (Ger., âr-hah′ben). Lofty, exalted.

Erklingen (Ger., âr-kling′en). To resound.

Ermattet (Ger., âr-măht′tet). Exhausted, wearied.

Ernst (Ger., ârnst). Earnest, grave.

Eroico,-a (It., ā-rôh′ē-kŏh, -kăh). Heroic; strong and dignified.

Erzählung (Ger., âr-tsä′lŏŏngᵏ). Story, tale, narration.

Es (Ger., ess). *E* flat.

Esclamato (It., ĕh-skăh-mah′tŏh). "Exclaimed"; forcibly declaimed.

Es dur (Ger., ess door). *E* flat major.

Eses (Ger., ess′ess). *E* double flat.

Es moll (Ger., ess mohl). *E* flat minor.

Espansivo (It., ĕh-spăhn-sē′vŏh). With intense feeling.

Espirando (It., ĕh-spă-răhn′dŏh). Dying away, expiring.

Espressivo (It., ĕh-spres-sē′vŏh). With expression, expressively.

Esquisse (Fr., es-keese′). A sketch.

Essential harmony. See HARMONY.

Estinguendo (It., ĕh-stin-gwen′dŏh). Extinguishing; dying away.

Estinto (It., ĕh-stin′tŏh). Barely audible; the extreme of *pianissimo*.

Etude (Fr., ā-tüd′). A study; especially one affording practice in some particular technical difficulty. . . *Étude de concert*, one designed for public performance.

Etwas (Ger., et′văhss). Rather, somewhat.

Euphonium. The bass saxhorn.

Eurhythmics. A system of musical training introduced by Jaques-Dalcroze in 1910 in which pupils were taught to represent complex rhythmic movement with their entire bodies, to the accompaniment of specially composed music.

Evensong. In the Anglican Church, a form of worship appointed to be said or sung at evening; known as Vespers in the Roman Catholic Church.

Execution. 1. Style, manner of performance.—2. Technical ability.

Exercise. A short technical study for training the fingers (or vocal organs) to overcome some special difficulty.—Also, a short study in composition.

Exposition. 1. The opening of a sonata movement, in which the principal themes are presented for the first time.—2. Sections of a fugue that present the subject.

Expressionism. An early 20th-century movement in music giving expression to the inner state of a composer's mind and emotion. Expressionism reflects anxious moods characteristic of modern life in a musical idiom using atonally constructed melodies and spasmodic, restless rhythms.

Expression mark. A written direction for the performance of a piece.

Extended compass. Tones beyond the usual range of a voice or instrument.

Extended harmony, interval. See OPEN HARMONY; INTERVAL.

Extension pedal. The loud (right) piano pedal.

F

F (Ger., *F*; Fr. and It. *fa*). The 4th tone and degree in the typical diatonic scale of *C* major. . *f* = *forte*, *ff* or *fff* = *fortissimo*.

Fa. 1. In solmization, the usual name for the 4th degree of the scale.— 2. Name of the tone *F* in Italy, France, Spain, and Russia.

Faburden. Old English term describing a progression in consecutive 6/3 chords, similar but not identical to Fauxbourdon.

Facile (Fr., făh-sēl′). Facile, easy, fluent.

Fado. A popular Portuguese song.

Fagott (Ger., făh-gŏht′), **Fagotto** (It., făh-gŏht′tŏh). Bassoon.

False relation. The chromatic contradiction of a tone in one part by sounding its chromatically altered octave in another part.

Falsetto. The highest of the vocal registers.

Fancy. Type of 17th-century English instrumental music. See FANTAISIE.

Fandango (Sp.). A lively dance in triple time for 2 dancers of opposite sex, who accompany it with castanets or tambourine.

Fanfare (fan′fâr). A flourish of trumpets or trumpet call.

Fantaisie (Fr., făhn-tä-zē′), **Fantasia** (It., făhn-tăh-zē′ăh), **Fantasie** (Ger., făhn-tăh- zē). 1. An improvisation.—2. An instrumental piece in free imitation (17th and 18th centuries);—3. A composition free in form and more or less fantastic in character; a Fantasy.—4. A potpourri or paraphrase.

Fantastico (It., făhn-tăh′stē-kŏh). Fantastic, fanciful.

Fastoso (It., făh-stoh′sŏh). Pompous, stately.

Fauxbourdon (Fr., foh-boor-dŭn). A contrapuntal technique of the 15th century, marked by parallel progressions in thirds and sixths. This practice eventually led to the use of consecutive 6/3 chords, common in classical usage.

F clef. The bass clef:

F dur (Ger., ĕff door). *F* major.

Feierlich (Ger., fī′er-lĭyh). Ceremonial, solemn, grave.

Fermata (It., fâr-mah′tăh). A hold: ⌢ ; a pause or interruption. See HOLD.

Ferne (Ger., fâr′nĕ). Distance. . . *Wie aus der Ferne*, as from a distance.

Feroce (It., fâ-roh′chĕh). Wildly, fiercely, vehemently.

Fes (Ger., fess). *F* flat.

Festspiel (Ger., fĕst′shpēl). A stage play in which music is included.

Feuerig (Ger., fahü´ĕ-rĭyh). With fire; fiery, impetuous.

F holes. The 2 *f*-shaped soundholes in the belly of the violin, etc.

Fiacco (It., fē-ăhk´kŏh). Languishing, feeble.

Fiato (It., fē-ah´tŏh). "Breath"; *stromentia fiato* are wind instruments.

Fiddle. A violin.

Fiero,-a (It., fē-â´rŏh, -räh). Wild, fierce; bold, vigorous.

Fife. An octave transverse flute with 6 holes and no keys; compass d^2 to d^4.

Fifteenth. A double octave. —Also, an organ stop of 2′ pitch.

Fifth. An interval of 5 diatonic degrees (see INTERVAL).—Also, the 5th degree in any diatonic scale; the Dominant. . . *False Fifth,* a diminished fifth.

Figuration. Rapid figures or phrases, containing passing and changing notes.

Figure. A group of notes in a melody.

Figured bass. The principal method of indicating the harmony to be used in the keyboard part in Baroque music, in which the bass line alone is given, annotated with numbers indicating the intervals to be used from the bass up, and thus determining the harmony. Also called thoroughbass or BASSO CONTINUO.

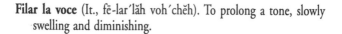

Filar la voce (It., fē-lar´läh voh´chĕh). To prolong a tone, slowly swelling and diminishing.

Filo di voce (It., fē´lŏh dē voh´chĕh). The very softest and lightest vocal tone.

Finale (It., fē-nah´lĕh). The last movement in a sonata or symphony; the closing number(s) of an act (opera) or Part (oratorio).

Fine (It., fē´nĕh). End; close; indicates either the end of a "repeat" (after the *Da capo* or *Dal segno*), or the end of a piece.

Fingering. 1. The method of applying the fingers to the keys, holes, strings, etc. of musical instruments.—2. The marks guiding the performer in finger placement.

Fingersatz (fin´ger-sähts). Fingering.

Fioritura (It., fē-oh-rē-too´räh). An embellishment; an ornamental turn, flourish, or phrase, introduced into a melody.

Fis (Ger., fiss). *F* sharp.

Fis dur (Ger., fiss door). *F* sharp major.

Fisis (Ger., fiss´iss). *F* double sharp.

Fis moll (Ger., fiss mohl). *F* sharp minor.

Fistel, Fistelstimme (Ger., fis´tel-shtim´mĕ). Falsetto.

47

Fixed Do. In the fixed Do system of solmization the tone *C*, and all its chromatic derivatives (*C♯*, *C♭*, *C×*, *C♭♭*), are called Do, *D* and its derivatives are called Re, etc., in whatever key or harmony they may appear.

Flag. A hook (♩) on the stem of a note.

Flageolet. A small vertical whistle flute. The French flageolet has a compass of 2 octaves and 3 semitones, from g^1 to $b^3♭$... *Flageolet tones*, Harmonics.

Flamenco. A Spanish or Gypsy dance characterized by vigorous heel stamping and passionate gesticulation.

Flat. The character ♭, which lowers the pitch of the note before which it is set by a semitone; the Double flat ♭♭ lowers its note by 2 semitones... *Flat fifth*, diminished fifth.

Flatterzunge (Ger., fläht-ter-tsoon'gheh). See FLUTTER-TONGUE.

Flautando (It., fläh-öö-tähn'döh), **Flautato** (It., fläh-öö-tah'töh). A direction in violin music to play near the fingerboard, so as to produce a somewhat "fluty" tone.

Flauto (It., fläh'öö-täh). Flute.

Flebile (It., flâ'bē-lĕh). Tearful; plaintive, mournful.

Fliessend (Ger., flē'sent). Flowing, smooth; *scorrendo*.

Florid. Embellished with runs, passages, figures, graces, etc.

Flourish. A trumpet fanfare.

Flüchtig (Ger., fl*ü*yh'tĭyh). Flightily, hastily; lightly, airily.

Flügelhorn. A brass instrument similar to but larger than the cornet.

Flute. The orchestral flute has a cylindrical metal tube with 14 vents closed by keys; it is blown through an oval orifice near the upper end. Normal compass is from c^1 to c^4. This is the so-called *transverse* or *cross flute*, being held across the mouth; the *vertical or direct flute* is blown from the end, like a whistle.

Flute à bec. RECORDER.

Flutter-tongue. A special effect in flute playing, done by trilling the tongue against the palate of the mouth. The effect can also be obtained by causing the uvula at the back of the mouth to vibrate.

F moll (Ger., ef mohl). *F* minor.

Folgend (Ger., fŏhl'ghent). "Following"; *colla parte* or *voce*.

Folia (Sp., fŏh-lē'äh). A Spanish dance for one person, in slow tempo and ¾ time.

Folk song. A song of the people, tinged by the musical peculiarities of the nation, and usually in simple, unaffected ballad form.

Foot. 1. A group of syllables having one accent like a simple measure in music.—2. The unit of measure in designating the pitch of organ stops and of the several octaves in the musical scale.

Forlana (It., fohr-lah´năh). A lively Italian dance in § or ¾ time.

Form. In music, a concept of organization governing the order, character, meter, and key of a composition. The most elementary form is binary, in which only 2 elements are presented. Ternary form evolves from binary by the interpolation of a middle section. In a large work, such as a sonata or symphony, formal elements often intermingle and are distinguished by their similarities or contrasts.

Forte (It., fôhr´těh). Loud, strong; usually written *f*; *piu forte*, louder; *piano forte* (*pf*), begin softly and swell rapidly; *poco forte*, rather loud; *forte piano* (*fp*), accent strongly, instantly diminishing to piano; *fortemente* (for-těh-měn´těh), loudly, forcibly; *forte possible* (pŏhs-sē´be-lěh), as loud as possible.

Fortepiano. A term used for the 18th-century piano to distinguish it from the modern instrument.

Fortissimo (It., fohr-tis´sē-mŏh). Extremely loud (usually written *ff*, or *fff*).

Forzato (It., fohr-tsah´tŏh). With force, energy; means that the note or chord is to be strongly accented; usually written *fz*

Four-hand piano. Pieces written for 2 piano players, one playing the treble parts and the other the bass.

Fourth. An interval embracing 4 degrees.—Also, the 4th degree in the diatonic scale; the subdominant.

Fox trot. A popular duple/quadruple metered ballroom dance that originated in the 1920s.

Free fugue. One written with more or less disregard of strict rules.

Free jazz. A JAZZ style of the 1960s–70s, characterized by collective improvisation without reference to present harmonic or formal structures.

Frei (Ger., frī). Free. . . *Frei im Vortrag*, free in style (delivery).

French horn. Spiral-shaped brass instrument with a tunnel-shaped opening. The modern French horn possesses a mellow tone capable of great expressive power.

French sixth. This is the common name for a chord containing the augmented sixth between the bottom and the top notes, other intervals from the bottom being a major third and an augmented fourth, as in *A* flat, *C, D,* and *F* sharp. See AUGMENTED SIXTH.

French overture. A type of 18th-century French overture consisting of 3 sections: the first in slow tempo, the second, rather quick and the third, again slow.

Fret. One of the narrow ridges of wood, metal, or ivory, crossing the fingerboard of the mandolin, guitar, zither, etc., on which the strings are "stopped."

Frettoloso (It., fret-tŏh-loh´sŏh). Hastily, hurriedly.

Freude (Ger., froy´-deh). Joy.

Frisch (Ger., frish). Brisk, vigorous; *brioso*.

Frog. Nut (of a bow).

Fröhlich (Ger., frö´lĭyh). Gay, glad, joyous.

Frosch (Ger., frŏsh). Nut (of a bow).

Frottola (It., froht´toh-lah). A type of choral madrigal popular in 16th-century Italy.

Fuga (L. and It., foo´găh). A fugue.

Fugato (It., fŏŏ-gah´tŏh; "in fugue style"). A passage or movement consisting of fugal imitations, but not worked out as a regular fugue.

Fuge (Ger., foo´gĕ). Fugue.

Fughetta (It., fŏŏ-get´tăh). A short fugue; a fugue exposition.

Fuging tune. A choral hymn with an imitative, though not truly fugal, section. Very popular in late 18th-century New England.

Fugue (fewg). The most highly developed form of contrapuntal imitation, based on the principle of the equality of the parts, a theme proposed by one part being taken up successively by all participating parts, thus bringing each in turn into special prominence.— The elements essential to every fugue are (1) the Subject, (2) the Answer, (3) Countersubject, (4) Stretto; to these are commonly added (5) Episodes, (6) an Organ point, (7) a Coda.

Fundamental. 1. The root of a chord.—2. A tone that produces a series of harmonics; a generator or fundamental bass. . . *Fundamental position*, any arrangements of chord-notes in which the root remains the lowest.

Funebre (It., fŏŏ´nâ-brĕh). Funereal, mournful, dirgelike.

Funeral march. A march in slow $\frac{4}{4}$ time in a minor key, sometimes used as a part of a larger work; the most famous funeral march is the slow movement from Chopin's piano sonata in *B*-flat minor.

Funky. A JAZZ style of the 1950s and 1960s that returns to the relative simplicities of BLUES; a reaction against the complexities of BEBOP and COOL.

Fuoco, con (It., kŏhn fŏŏ-ô´kŏh). With fire, fiery, spirited.

Furioso (It., foo-rē-oh´sŏh). Furiously, wildly.

Furore (It., foo-roh´rĕh). Fury, passion; a rage, mania. . . *Con furore*, passionately.

Futurism. A literary and musical modern movement that originated in Italy early in the 20th century. It declared a rebellion against traditional art of all kinds, and preached the use of noises in musical composition.

G

G. The fifth tone and degree in the typical diatonic scale of *C* major... G. stands for *gauche* in *m.g. (main gauche,* left hand); G. O. for *Grand-orgue* (Great organ).

Gagliarda (It., găhl-yar´dăh). A GALLIARD.

Gai (Fr., gä). Gay, lively, brisk.

Galant (Fr., gah-lan´). Gallant; *Style galant* was the description of the light style of composition popular in France in the late 18th century.

Galliard. An old French dance for 2 dancers, gay and spirited, but not rapid, and in ¾ time.

Galop (Fr., găh-lŏh´). A lively round dance in 2/4 time.

Gamba (It., gahm´băh). A viola da gamba.

Gamelan. A typical instrumental orchestra of Indonesia, primarily composed of percussion instruments, although some ensembles also use reeds and strings.

Gamme (Fr., găhm). A scale.

Gamut. 1. The scale.—2. The staff.

Ganz (Ger., găhnts). 1. Whole; *ganze Note,* whole note.—2. Very; *ganz langsam,* very slowly.

Garbato (gar-bah´tŏh). Gracefully, elegantly; in a refined style.

Gathering note. In chanting, a hold on the last syllable of the recitation.

Gauche (Fr., gohsh). Left.

Gavotte (Fr., găh-vŏht). An old French dance in strongly marked duple time (*alla breve*), beginning on the upbeat.

G dur (Ger., gā door). *G* major.

Gebrauchsmusik (Ger., gĕ-browhs´moo-zĭk). "Utility music," music for amateur use.

Gebunden (Ger., gĕ-bŏŏn´den). Tied; *legato.*

Gedämpft (Ger., gĕ-dempft´). Damped; muffled; muted.

Gedehnt (Ger., gĕ-dānt´). Sustained, prolonged; slow, stately.

Gefällig (Ger., gĕ-fel´lĭyh). Pleasing, graceful.

Gefühlvoll (Ger., gĕ-fül´fŏhl). With feeling, expressively.

Gehalten (Ger., gĕ-hăhl´ten). Held, sustained.

Gehaucht (Ger., gĕ-howht´). "Sighed"; very softly and lightly sung or played.

Geheimnisvoll (Ger., gĕ-hīm´nĭs-fŏhl). Mysterious.

Gehend (Ger., gā´ent). Andante.

Geige (Ger., gī´gĕ). Violin.

Geist (Ger., gīst). Spirit, soul; essence.

Gelassen (Ger., gĕ-lăhs´sĕn). Calm, placid, easy.

Geläufig (Ger., gĕ-lăhü´fǐyh). Fluent, easy. . . *Geläufigkeit,* fluency, velocity.

Gemächlich (Ger., gĕ-mĕyh´lǐyh). Easy, comfortable.

Gemässigt (Ger., gĕ-mä´sǐyht). Moderate (in tempo).

Gemessen (Ger., gĕ-mes´sen). Measured(ly), moderate(ly); *moderato.*

Gemischte Stimmen (Ger., gĕ-mǐsh´te shtǐ´mmen). Mixed voices.

Gemüt(h)lich (Ger., gĕ-m*üt*´lǐyh). Easily and cheerily.

Generalbass (Ger., gĕh-nĕh-rahl´băhs). Basso continuo.

Generalpause (Ger., gĕh-nĕh-rahl´pow´-zŭ). A rest for an entire orchestra.

Generoso (It., jĕh-nĕh-roh´sŏh). Free, ample.

Gentile (It., jen-tē´lĕh). In a graceful, refined style.

German sixth. A chord of the augmented sixth between the bottom and the top notes. Other intervals from the bottom are a major third and a perfect fifth, as in *A* flat, *C, E* flat, *F* sharp. See Augmented sixth.

Ges (Ger., gess). *G* flat.

Gesang (Ger., gĕ-zăhngᵏ´). Singing, song; a song; melody; voice (vocal part).

Geschleift (Ger., gĕ-shlīft´). Slurred; *legato.*

Geschmackvoll (Ger., gĕ-shmăhk´fŏhl). Tastefully.

Geschwindt (Ger., gĕ-shvint´). Swift(ly), rapid(ly).

Ges dur (Ger., gĕs door). *G* flat major.

Geses (Ger., gess´ess). *G* double flat.

Gestopft (Ger., gĕ-shtŏ´pft). Stopped. Modifying the tone of a horn by inserting the hand into the bell of the instrument, thus raising the tone a half step.

Gestossen (Ger., gĕ-shtŏh´sen). 1. Staccato.—2. Détaché.

Geteilt (Ger., gĕ-tīl´t). Divided.

Getragen (Ger., gĕ-trah´gen). Sustained, *sostenuto.*

Gigue (Fr., zhig). A Jig.

52

Giocoso, -a (It., jŏh-koh´sŏh, -săh). Playfully, sportively, merrily.

Gis (Ger., giss). *G* sharp.

Gisis (Ger., gĭss´ĭs). *G* double sharp.

Gis moll (Ger., mohl). *G* sharp minor.

Giubilante (It., joo-bē-lăhn´těh). Jubilant.

Giusto (It., jŏŏ´ stŏh). Strict, appropriate, proper (*tempo giusto*), exact, correct.—*Allegro giusto*, moderately fast.

Glass harmonica. A set of glasses of different sizes that are rubbed on the rim with wet fingers producing a gentle ethereal sound.

Glee. A secular composition for 3 or more unaccompanied solo voices, peculiar to England. Serious "glees" are written as well as merry ones.

Gli (It., l'yē). The (masculine plural).

Glissando (It., glis-săhn'dŏh). 1. On bowed instruments, *(a)* a flowing, unaccented execution of a passage; *(b)* same as PORTAMENTO.—2. On the piano, a rapid scale effect obtained by sliding the thumb, or thumb and one finger, over the keys.

Glocke (Ger., glŏh´kě). A bell.

Glockenspiel (Ger., glŏh´ken-shpēl´). A set of bells or steel bars, tuned diatonically and struck with a small hammer.

Glottis. The aperture between the vocal cords when they are drawn together in singing.

G

G moll (Ger., gä mohl). *G* minor.

Gong. A suspended circular metal plate, struck with a mallet and producing a sustained reverberation.

Goose. A harsh break in the tone of the clarinet, oboe, or bassoon.

Gospel song. A Protestant church hymn.

G. P. Abbreviation for GENERALPAUSE.

Grace. An ornament not essential to the melody or harmony of a composition.

Grace note. A note of embellishment, usually written small.

Gradatamente (It., grăh-dăh-tăh-men´těh). By degrees, gradually.

Gradevole (grăh-dā´vŏh-lěh). Pleasingly, agreeably.

Gradual. 1. An antiphon following the epistle.—2. A book of chants containing the graduals, introits, and other antiphons of the Roman Catholic Mass.

Gramophone. A trademark commonly used in England for the phonograph.

Gran cassa (It., grähn cah´säh). Bass drum; literally, "big box."

Grand (Fr., grähn). Large, great; full. . . *Grand barré*, a stop of over 3 notes.

Grande (It. grähn´dëh). Large, great, full. *Grande* is the regular form, used after nouns; it is abbreviated to *grand'* before vowels, and to *gran* before consonants.

Grandioso (It., grähn-dë-oh´söh). With grandeur; majestically, pompously, loftily.

Grand opera. A type of opera, usually in 5 acts, treating a heroic, mythological, or historical subject, sumptuously costumed, and produced in a large opera house.

Grave (It., grah´vëh). 1. Low in pitch.—2. Heavy, slow, ponderous in movement.—3. Serious.

Gravicembalo (It., gräh-vë-chëm-bahl´oh). Harpsichord.

Grazioso, -a (It., gräh-tsë-oh´söh, -säh). Gracefully, elegantly.

Great octave. Common name for the octave beginning on *C*, two leger lines below the staff of the bass clef.

Great organ. The chief manual of an organ, and the pipes controlled by it.

Gregorian chant. Plainchant as revised and established by Pope Gregory I (d. 604).

G

Grosso (It., grô´söh). Great, grand; full, heavy.

Ground bass. A continually repeated bass phrase of 4 or 8 measures.

Group. 1. A short series of rapid notes, especially when sung to one syllable—2. A section of the orchestra (or score) embracing instruments of one class.

Gruppetto (It., grööp-pet´pöh). Formerly, a trill; now, a turn; also, any "group" of grace notes. Also called *Gruppo*.

G string. The lowest string on the violin. On the viola and cello it is the second string above the lowest string; on the double bass it is the highest string.

Guitar. An instrument of the lute family. The modern Spanish guitar has 6 strings, and a compass of 3 octaves and a Fourth, from *E* to *a* [2]. The music is written an octave higher than it sounds, in the *G* clef.

Gusli. An ancient Russian zither-type instrument.

Gusto (It., göö´stöh). Taste.

Gut (Ger., goot). Good.

H

H. In scores, H stands for *Horn*; in keyboard music, for *Hand* (*r.h.*, *l.h.*).

H (Ger., hah). The note *B*.

Habanera (Sp., hăh-băh-nâ´răh). A Cuban dance, in duple meter, characterized by dotted or syncopated rhythms.

Halb (Ger., hăhlp). Half.

Half note. A note one-half the value of a whole note and represented by a white circle with a stem. (♩).

Half step. A semitone.

Hallelujah (Hebr.). "Praise ye the Lord!"

Hammerclavier (Ger., hăhm´mer-klăh-vēr´). Old name for the Piano.

Harfe (Ger., har´fĕ). Harp.

Harmonic. 1. (*adjective*). Pertaining to chords and to the theory and practice of harmony. . . *H. figuration*, in music for violin, etc., a sign (○) over a note, calling for a harmonic tone. . . *H. scale*, (a) the succession of harmonic tones; (b) minor scale with minor Sixth and major Seventh. . . 2. (*noun*). (a) One of the series of tones (the so-called *partial tones*) that usually accompany, more or less faintly, the prime tone produced by a string, an organ pipe, the human voice, etc. The *prime tone* (*fundamental*) is the strong tone produced by the vibration of the whole string, or the entire column of air in the pipe; the *partial* tones are produced by the vibration of fractional parts of that string or air column. (b) These same harmonics are obtained, on any string instrument that is stopped (violin, zither), by lightly touching a nodal point of a string.

Harmonica. Also called mouth harmonica or mouth organ. A set of graduated metal reeds mounted in a narrow frame, blown by the mouth, and producing different tones on expiration and inspiration.

Harmonie. French term for wind instruments.

Harmonic series. A natural series of overtones, sounding an octave above the fundamental tone, then a fifth higher, a fourth higher, a major third higher, a minor third higher, etc. The first 6 members of the natural harmonic series form the harmony of the major triad, fundamental to all acoustic phenomena.

Harmonisch (Ger., har-moh´nish). Harmonic (*adj.*); harmonious.

Harmonium. A portable organ, activated by 2 pedals with both feet operating one after another to pump the air.

Harmony. 1. A musical combination of tones or chords.—2. A chord, either consonant or dissonant.—3. The harmonic texture of a piece; as 2-part, 3-part harmony. . . *Chromatic harmony* has chromatic tones and modulations. . . *Close harmony* (in 4-part writing) has the 3 highest parts within the compass of an octave. . . *Compound harmony* has 2 or more essential chord-tones doubled. . . *Essential harmony*, (a) the fundamental triads of a key; *(b)* the harmonic frame of a composition minus all figuration and ornaments. . . *False harmony, (a)* the inharmonic relation; *(b)* discord produced by imperfect preparation or resolution; *(c)* discord produced by wrong notes or chords. . . *Figured harmony* varies the simple chords by figuration of all kinds. . . *Open harmony* (in 4-part writing) spreads the 3 highest parts beyond the compass of an octave.

Harp. A string instrument of ancient origin. The modern orchestral harp has a nearly 3-cornered wooden *frame*, the *foot* of which is formed by an upright *pillar* meeting the hollow *back* (the upper side of which bears the *soundboard*) in the *pedestal;* the upper ends of pillar and back are united by the curving *neck.* The gut strings are 46 or (47) in number. Compass, 6½ octaves, from $C_1\flat$ to $f^4\flat$ (or $g^4\flat$).

Harpsichord. A keyboard string instrument in which the strings are twanged by quills or bits of hard leather.

Haupt (Ger., howpt). Head; chief, principal. . . *Hauptmanual,* Great-organ manual. . . *Hauptsatz,* principal movement or theme.

Hautbois (Fr., ŏh-bwăh´). Oboe.

H dur (Ger., hah door). *B* major.

Head. 1. Point (of bow). —2. In the violin, etc., the part comprising peg-box and scroll.—3. In the drum, the membrane stretched over one or both ends.—4. In a note, the oval (or square) part that determines its place on the staff.

Head tones, Head voice. The vocal tones of the head register.

Heckelphone. A baritone oboe with a range an octave below the oboe.

Heftig (Ger., hef´tǐyh). Vehement, impetuous, passionate.

Heimlich (Ger., hǐm´lǐyh). Secret, mysterious; furtive, stealthy.

Heiter (Ger., hī´ter). Serene; cheerful, glad; *gioioso.*

H

Heldentenor. In German, "heroic tenor," requiring a robust voice for difficult operatic parts, particularly in Wagner's music dramas.

Helicon. A brass wind instrument, used chiefly in military music as a bass; its tube is bent in a circle, and it is carried over the shoulder.

Hell (Ger., hel). Clear, bright.

Hemidemisemiquaver. A sixty-fourth note.

Hemiola. In mensural notation of the Middle Ages, the use of 3 notes of equal value in the same bar length, so that the longer notes equal 1½ shorter ones. In modern notation the hemiola is represented by a succession of ⅜ and ¾ bars.

Hervorgehoben (Ger., hâr-fŏhr´gĕ-hō´ben). Emphasized.

Hervortretend (Ger., hâr-fŏhr´trā-tent). A term indicating that the part to which it is applied is to be brought to the fore, in contrast to the accompanying parts.

Herzig (Ger., hâr'tsĭyh). Hearty, heartily; tenderly.

Hexachord. The 6 tones *ut re mi fa sol la* in Solmization.

Hidden fifths, octaves. Progressions of intervals leading towards an open fifth, or an octave, from the same direction, forbidden in strict harmony.

His (Ger., hiss). *B* sharp.

H moll (Ger., hĭss mohl). *B* minor.

Hochzeitlied (Ger., hōh'-tsīt-lēt). Wedding song.

Hocket. A medieval contrapuntal device in which one voice stops and another voice comes in, sometimes in the middle of a word, creating the effect of hiccuping.

Hold. The sign ⌒ over, or ⌣ under, a note or rest, indicating the prolongation of its time value at the performer's discretion.— Placed over a bar, the hold indicates a slight pause before attacking what follows. See FERMATA.

Homophonic. Music in which one melody or part, supported to a greater or less extent by chords or chordal combinations (that is, an *accompanied melody*); opposed to *polyphonic*.

Horn. The orchestral horn (*French horn*) is a brass wind instrument, having a conical tube variously bent upon itself (the smallest horn generally used, in high *B*, has a tube nearly 9 feet long; that an octave lower, nearly 18 feet); wide and flaring bell; the tone rich, mellow, and sonorous. The old *natural horn* yields only the natural tones supplemented by stopped tones and crooks, giving a total possible compass of 3½ octaves, from $B_i\flat$ to f.—The modern *Valve-horn*, played like a cornet, is much easier to handle.— The horn is a transposing instrument.

Hornpipe. An old English dance in lively tempo, the earlier ones in $\frac{3}{2}$ time, the later in $\frac{4}{4}$ time.

Humoresque. A light, whimsical instrumental piece, often for piano.

Hurdy-gurdy. A string instrument having 2 melody strings, and from 2 to 4 drones. The melody strings are "stopped" by keys touched by the left hand; the right hand turns a crank that revolves a rosined wheel, the latter scraping the strings and producing the rough musical tones.

Hurtig (Ger., hŏŏr'tĭyh). Swift, headlong.

Hydraulic organ. A small kind of organ invented by Ktesibios of Alexandria (180 B.C.), in which the wind pressure was regulated by water.

Hymn. A religious or sacred song; usually, a metrical poem to be sung by a congregation.—Also, a national song of lofty character, like the *Marseillaise*.

Hypo-. In the system of church modes, the prefix *hypo-* indicates the starting point of a mode a fourth below its tonic.

H

I

I (It., ē; *masculine plural*). The.

Iambus. A metrical foot of 2 syllables, one short and one long, with the accent on the long: ˘ ‒.

Ictus. A separation mark in Gregorian chant before and after an important note in the melody; in poetic usage, *ictus* means a "stress."

Idée fixe. In French, "fixed idea"; a term used by Berlioz in his *Fantastic Symphony* for the recurrent theme in the work.

Idyl. A composition of a pastoral or tenderly romantic character, without set form.

Il (It., ēl; *masculine singular*). The. . . *Il più*, the most.

Im (Ger., im). In the. . . *Im Tempo*, in the regular tempo; *a tempo*.

Imitation. The repetition of a motive, phrase, or theme proposed by one part (the antecedent) in another part (the consequent), with or without modification. . . *Canonic imitation*, strict imitation. . . *Free imitation,* that in which changes of the antecedent are permitted in the consequent.. . *Strict imitation,* that in which the consequent answers the antecedent note for note and interval for interval.

Immer (Ger., im′mer). Always; continuously.

Imperfect cadence, consonance, interval. See the nouns.

Imponente (It., im-pŏh-nen′tĕh). Imposing, impressive.

Impressionism. A term used to describe early 20th-century French composition, in which subtle impressions rather than programmatic descriptions are conveyed through use of ethereal harmonies in free modulation and colorful instrumentation.

Impromptu. A composition of loose and extemporaneous form and slight development; a Fantasia.

Improvisation. Creating or extemporizing music while performing it.

Incalzando (It., in-kăhl-tsăhn′dŏh). "Pursuing hotly"; growing more vehement. . . *Incalzando e stringendo,* growing more vehement and rapid.

Incidental music. Music supplementary to a spoken drama; such as an overture, interludes, songs, etc.

Indeciso (It., in-dĕh-chē′sŏh). Irresolute, undecided.

Independent chord, harmony, triad. One that is consonant (contains no dissonance), and is, therefore, not obliged to change to another chord by progression or resolution.

Indirect resolution. See RESOLUTION.

Infinite canon. One without a closing cadence, that may be repeated at pleasure.

Infino (It., in-fē'nŏh). Up to, as far as, till you reach.

Inharmonic relation. See FALSE RELATION.

Inner parts. Parts in harmony lying between the highest and lowest.

Inner pedal. A pedal point on an inner part.

Innig (Ger., in'nĭyh). Heartfelt, sincere, fervent, intense; *intimo, con affetto.*

Inquieto (It., in-kwē-ĕh'tŏh). Unrestful, uneasy.

Insensibile (It., in-sen-sē'bē-lĕh). Imperceptible.

Instrumentation. The theory and practice of composing, arranging, or adapting music for a body of instruments of different kinds, especially for orchestra.

Interlude. 1. An intermezzo.—2. An instrumental strain or passage connecting the lines or stanzas of a hymn, etc.—3. An instrumental piece played between certain portions of the church service (*Interludium*).

Intermezzo (in-tĕr-med'zŏh). 1. A light musical entertainment alternating with the acts of the early Italian tragedies.—2. Incidental music in modern dramas.—3. A short movement connecting the main divisions of a symphony.

Interval. The difference in pitch between two tones. Intervals are regularly measured from the lower tone to the higher. An interval is:—*Augmented,* when wider by a chromatic semitone than major or perfect. . . *Chromatic,* when augmented or diminished (except aug. fourth and dim. fifth and seventh). . . *Compound,* when wider than an octave. . . *Consonant,* when not requiring resolution. . . *Diatonic,* when occurring between 2 tones belonging to the same key (except the augmented second and fifth of the harmonic minor scale). . . *Diminished,* when a chromatic semitone narrower than major or perfect. . . *Dissonant,* when requiring resolution. . . *Extended,* when augmented. . . *Flat,* when diminished. . . *Harmonic,* when both tones are sounded together. . . *Imperfect,* when diminished. . . *Inverted,* when the higher tone is lowered, or the lower tone raised, by an octave. . . *Major,* when equal to the standard second, third, sixth, and seventh of the major scale. . . *Minor,* when a chromatic semitone narrower than major or perfect. . . *Parallel* (with an interval preceding), when its two tones progress in the same direction and at the same interval. . . *Perfect* (or *Perfect major*), when equal to the standard prime, fourth, fifth, and octave of the major scale. . . *Simple,* when not wider than an octave.

Intonation. 1. The production of tone.—2. The method of chanting employed in Plainchant.—3. The opening notes leading up to the reciting tone of a chant.

Intrada (It., in-trăh'dăh). A short introduction or prelude.

Introduction. A phrase or division preliminary to and preparatory of a composition or movement.

Introit (L., ĭn-trō ´ĭt, "entrance"). An antiphon sung while the priest is approaching the altar to celebrate the Mass.—In the modern Anglican Church, an anthem or psalm, sung as the minister approaches the Communion table.

Invention. A short piece in free contrapuntal style, developing one motive in an impromptu fashion.

Inversion. The transposition of the notes of an interval or chord. *(a)* In a simple interval the higher note is set an octave lower, or the lower note an octave higher. *(b)* A chord is *inverted* when its lowest note is not the root. *(c)* In double counterpoint, the transposition of 2 parts, the higher being set below the lower, or vice versa; this inversion may be by an octave or some other interval, and is called "inversion in the octave," "in the fifth," etc. *(d)* A melody is inverted when ascending intervals are made to descend by the same degree, and vice versa. The melody is therefore turned upside down.

Invertible counterpoint. A type of polyphonic writing in which contrapuntal parts could be inverted and placed in different voices without forming forbidden discords. Also called DOUBLE COUNTERPOINT.

Ionian mode. An ecclesiastical mode corresponding to a major scale.

Irregular cadence. See CADENCE.

Isorhythm. In the 14th and 15th centuries, a technique using a repeated pitch pattern (COLOR) and a repeated rhythmic pattern (TALEA). The color and talea do not necessarily coincide, so that the repeated pitches are presented in different rhythms and phrases.

Italian overture. An overture current in the 17th-18th centuries consisting of 3 sections—quick, slow, and quick—in contradistinction to the French overture in which the sections are slow, quick, and slow.

Italian sixth. A chord of three notes, containing the augmented sixth from bottom to top and a major third from bottom to the middle note, as in *A* flat, *C*, and *F* sharp. See AUGMENTED SIXTH.

J

Jack. 1. In the harpsichord and clavichord, an upright slip of wood on the rear end of the key lever, to which the *plectrum* is fixed.— 2. In the piano, the escapement lever, or hopper.

Jagdhorn (Ger., yăht´horn). Hunting horn.

Jägerchor (Ger., yä´ger-kohr´). Hunters' chorus.

Janizary music. Turkish military music, with drums, cymbals, etc., predominating.

Jazz. A term covering a variety of styles of black American origin: RAGTIME, BLUES, DIXIELAND, SWING, BEBOP, COOL, THIRD STREAM, FREE JAZZ, FUNKY, and other less definable styles. Most are characterized by improvisation and a "swinging beat" composed of a steady, prominent meter and dotted or syncopated rhythms.

Jew's harp. A small instrument with rigid iron frame, having a thin vibratile metal tongue; the frame is held between the teeth, and the metallic tongue plucked with the finger.

Jig. A kind of country dance, with many modifications of step and gesture, in triple or compound time, and rapid tempo.—In the Suite, the *Gigue* is usually the last movement.

Jingling Johnny. A percussion instrument, consisting of a stick overhung with jingles and bells. It is also known as a Turkish Crescent or Chinese Pavilion.

Jongleur (Fr., zhon-glör´). A medieval minstrel employed by royalty and aristocracy to provide light entertainment.

Jota (Sp., hoh´tăh). A national dance of northern Spain, danced by couples, in triple time and rapid movement, something like a waltz.

Just intonation. Singing or playing music precisely true to pitch; opposed to tempered intonation.

J

K

Kammer (Ger., kăhm′mer). "Chamber"; "court"; *Kammermusik*, chamber music; *Kammermusiker*, court musician; *Kammerkantate*, chamber cantata.

Kantate (Ger., kăhn-tah′tĕ). Cantata.

Kantele. National Finnish instrument, plucked with fingers like a zither.

Kapelle (Ger., kăh-pel′lĕ). 1. A private band or choir.—2. An orchestra.

Kapellmeister (Ger., kăh-pel′mīs′ter).1. Orchestra conductor.—2. Choirmaster.

Kazoo. A toy-like instrument consisting of a short tube with membranes at each end, into which the player hums, producing a curiously nasal tone.

Kettledrum. See Timpani.

Key (1). The series of tones forming any given major or minor scale, considered with reference to their harmonic relations, particularly the relation of the other tones to the tonic or keynote. . . *Attendant keys*, see Attendant. . . *Chromatic key*, one having sharps or flats in the signature. . . *Major key*, one having a major Third and Sixth. . . *Minor key*, one having a minor Third and Sixth. . . *Natural key*, one with neither sharps nor flats in the signature. . . *Parallel* key, *(a)* a minor key with the same keynote as the given major key, or vice versa, *(b)* a *Relative key* (see Relative). . . *Remote key*, an indirectly related key. (2). *(a)* A digital or finger lever in the keyboard of a piano or organ.—*(b)* A pedal or foot key in the organ or pedal piano. (3). A flat padded disk attached to a lever worked by the finger or thumb, closing the soundholes of various wind instruments. (4). A wrest, or tuning key.

Keyboard. The range of keys on an organ or piano.

Key bugle. See Bugle.

Key signature. The sharps or flats at the head of the staff.

Kirchenmusik (Ger., kĭryh′en-moo-zĭk). Church music.

Kithara. An ancient Greek instrument of the lyre family, with several strings stretched over the soundbox.

Klagend (Ger., klah′ghent). Mournfully, plaintively.

Klang (Ger., klăng^k). 1. A sound.—2. A composite musical tone (a fundamental tone with its harmonics).—3. A chord, as in *Dreiklang*—triad.

Klangfarbe (Ger., klăng^k′far-bĕ). Tone color.

Klangfarbenmelodie (Ger., klăng^k-fahr-běn-mel´oh-dē). A technique of the 20th- century Viennese school in which tone colors are treated like melodies.

Klappe (Ger., klăhp´pě). A key (3). . . *Klappenhorn*, key bugle.

Klarinette (Ger., klăh-rē-net´tě). Clarinet.

Klavier (Ger., klăh-vēr´). 1. A keyboard.—2. A keyboard string instrument; in the 18th century, a clavichord; now, a piano of any kind.

Knabenstimme (Ger., knăh´běn-shtĭ´mě). A boy's voice.

Konzert (Ger., köhn-tsârt´). 1. Concerto.—2. Concert.

Konzertmeister (Ger., köhn-tsârt´mī-ster). Concertmaster.

Konzertstück (Ger., köhn-tsârt´shtük). 1. A concert piece.—2. A short concerto in 1 movement and free form.

Koto. Japanese string instrument similar to a zither.

Kräftig (Ger., kref´tǐyh). Forceful, vigorous, energetic; *con forza*.

Krebsgang (Ger., krĕps´găhng). Literally, "crab walk"; a retrograde motion of a given theme or passage.

Kreuz (Ger., kroytz). The sharp sign (♯).

Krummhorn (Ger., krŏŏm´horn). An obsolete double-reed instrument.

Kurz (Ger., kŏŏrts). Short. . . *Kurz und bestimmt*, short and decided.

Kyrie (Gk., kü´rē-ĕh). "Lord"; the first word in the opening division of the Mass.

L

L. Stands for *left* (or *links,* Ger.) in the direction *l.h.* (left hand).

La. 1. The 6th Aretinian syllable.—2. The note *A* in French and Italian.—3. (It., läh). The.

Lacrimosa (L. läh-crē-möh´zäh). A part of the Requiem Mass.

Lage (Ger., lah´gĕ). Position (of a chord); position, shift (in violin playing). . . *Enge (weite) Lage,* close (open) position or harmony.

Lah stands for *La* in Tonic Sol-fa.

Lamentoso (It., läh-men-toh´söh). Lamentingly, plaintively, mournfully.

Ländler (Ger., lent´ler). A slow waltz of South Germany and the Tyrol, in ¾ or ⅜ time, and the rhythm

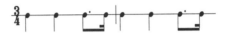

Langsam (Ger., lähngᵏ´zähm). Slow. . . *Langsamer,* slower.

Largamente (It., lar-gäh-men´tĕh). Largely, broadly.

Largando (It., lar-gähn´döh). "Growing broader"; that is, slower and more marked; generally a *crescendo* is implied.

Large. A Plainchant note equal to 2 (or 3) longs.

Larghetto (It. lar-get´töh). The diminutive of *Largo,* it demands a somewhat more rapid tempo, nearly *Andantino.*

Largo (It., lar´göh). Large, broad; the slowest tempo mark, calling for a slow and stately movement with ample breadth of style. . . *Largo assai,* very slowly and broadly (also *Largo di molto, Molto largo,* or *Larghissimo*). . . *Poco largo,* "with some breath"; can occur even during an Allegro.

Lauda (Latin). A laud (hymn or song of praise). . . *Laudes,* lauds; together with matins, the first of the 7 Canonical Hours.

Laudamus te. "We praise Thee"—part of the Gloria of the Mass.

Laudi spirituali. Medieval songs of devotion.

Laute (Ger., low´tĕ). Lute.

Lay. A melody or tune.

Le (It., lā; Fr., lŭ). The.

Lead. 1. The giving-out or proposition of a theme by one part.—2. A cue.

Leader. 1. Conductor, director.—2. In the orchestra, the 1st violin; in a band, the 1st cornet; in a mixed chorus, the 1st soprano.—3. An antecedent.

Leading. 1. (*noun*). The melodic progrression or conduct of any part.—2. (*adjective*). Principal, chief; guiding, directing. . . *Leading* chord, the dominant seventh chord. . . *Leading melody*, principal melody or theme. . . *Leading motive*, see LEITMOTIV. . . *Leading note, tone*, the 7th degree of the major and harmonic minor scales.

Leaning note. Appoggiatura.

Leap. 1. In piano playing, a spring from one note or chord to another.—2. In harmony, a skip.

Lebhaft (Ger., läb´hähft). Lively, animated. . . *Lebhaft, aber nicht zu sehr*, lively, but not too much so.

Ledger line. A short line used for writing notes that lie above or below the staff. . . *Ledger space*, a space bounded on either side or both sides by a ledger line.

Legatissimo (It., lěh-gǐh-tǐs´sē-mŏh). Very smoothly and evenly. On the piano, in passages marked *legatissimo*, each finger is to hold its note as long as possible.

Legato (It., lěh-gah´tŏh). Bound, slurred; a direction to perform the passage in a smooth and connected manner, with no break between the tones; also indicated by the "legato mark," a curving line under or over notes to be so executed.

Legend. A composition depicting the course of a short tale of legendary character.

Leggero (It., led-jâ´roh). Light, airy.

Leggiadro (It., led-jah´drŏh). Neat, elegant, graceful.

Legno, col (It., kŏhl län´yŏh). "With the stick"; let the stick of the bow fall on the strings.

Leicht (Ger., līyht). Light, brisk; easy, facile. . . *Leicht bewegt*, lightly and swiftly; with slight agitation.

Leidenschaftlich (Ger., lī´den-shähft´lǐyh). With passion; passionately.

Leidvoll (Ger., līt´fŏhl). Sorrowful, mournful.

Leise (Ger., lī´zě). Low, soft; *piano*.

Leitmotiv (Ger., līt´mŏh-tēf´). Leading motive; any striking musical motive (theme, phrase) characterizing or accompanying one of the actors in a drama, or some particular idea, emotion, or situation in the latter.

Leno (It., lä´nŏh). Faint, gentle, quiet.

Lento (It., len´tŏh). Slow; calls for a tempo between *andante* and *largo*. . . *Adagio no lento*, slowly, but not dragging.

Lesson. English keyboard piece of the 17th and 18th centuries.

Lesto (It., lâ´stŏh). Gay, lively, brisk.

Liberamente (It., lē-běh-rǎh-men´těh). Freely, boldly.

Libretto (It., lē-bret′tŏh). A "booklet"; the words of an opera, oratorio, etc.

Licenza (It., lē-chen′tsäh). Freedom, license. . . *Con alcuna licenza*, with a certain degree of freedom.

Lieblich (Ger., lēp′lĭyh). Lovely, sweet, charming.

Lied (Ger., leed). A song, particularly an art song; the plural is *lieder*.

Liedertafel. A general name for a German male choral society.

Ligature. 1. A tie; a syncopation.—2. A group or series of notes to be executed in one breath, to one syllable, or as a legato phrase.

Light opera. An operetta.

Linear counterpoint. A modern term describing a type of contrapuntal writing in which individual lines are the main considerations in the ensemble.

Lip. 1. The upper and lower lips of a flue pipe are the flat surfaces above and below the mouth.—2. Lipping; that is, the art of so adjusting the lips to the mouthpiece of a wind instrument as to get a good tone.

Lirico. Italian word for *lyric*.

Liscio (It., lē′shŏh). Smooth, flowing.

L'istesso tempo (It., lē-stes′sŏh tem-pŏh). The same tempo.

Litany. A song of supplication, priests and choir alternating.

Liturgy. The total service of the Christian church.

Liuto (It., lē-oo′tŏh). A lute.

Lo (It., loh). The.

Lobgesang (Ger., lŏhb′gĕ-sängᵏ). Song of praise.

Loco (It., lô′kŏh). "Place"; following 8*va* it means "perform the notes as written."

Locrian mode. An ecclesiastical mode based on the 7th degree of the major scale.

Long. A Plainchant note equal to 2 (or 3) breves.

Lontano (It., lŏhn-tah′nŏh). Far away. . . *Da lontano*, from a distance.

Loud pedal. The piano pedal that lifts the dampers; the right pedal.

Lourd (Fr., loor). Heavy.

Louré (Fr., loorā). Slurred, legato, *non staccato*.

Luftig (Ger., lŏŏf′tĭyh). Airy, light.

Lugubre (It., lŏŏ-goo′brĕh). Mournful.

Lunga (It., lŏŏn´gah). Long; sustained. Written over or under a hold (⌢) it means that the pause is to be quite prolonged; often written *Pausa lunga*, long pause.

Lur. A primitive wooden trumpet in use by shepherds in Scandinavia.

Lusingando (It., loo-zin-gähn´dŏh). Coaxingly, caressingly, flatteringly, seductively.

Lustig (Ger., lŏŏs´tïyh). Merry, merrily.

Lute. A general term for a variety of plucked string instruments.

Luthier. (Fr., leu-tieh´). A maker of lutes and other string instruments.

Luttuoso (It., lŏŏt-tŏŏ-oh´sŏh). Mournful, doleful, plaintive.

Lydian mode. The church mode that begins on the fourth note of the major scale.

Lyre. An ancient Greek string instrument, the body being a soundboard, from which rise 2 curving arms joined above by a crossbar; the strings, from 3 to 10 in number, stretch from this crossbar to or over a bridge set on the soundboard, and are plucked with a plectrum.

Lyric, lyrical. Adapted for singing, or for expression in song; opposed to *epic* (narrative) and *dramatic* (scenic). . . *Lyric drama*, the opera. . . *Lyric opera*, one in which the lyric form predominates. . . *Lyric stage*, the operatic stage.

Lyrics. The text of a popular song or of a musical.

M

M. Stands for It., *mano* or Fr., *main* (hand); for *Manual* (organ); and for *Metronome.*

Ma (It., măh). But. . . *Allegro ma non troppo,* rapidly, but not too fast.

Mächtig (Ger., mäyh´tǐyh). Powerful, mighty.

Madrigal. A short lyric poem or vocal setting of such a poem in from 3 to 8 parts, contrapuntal, and usually for unaccompanied chorus; there are also madrigals in simple harmony, in dance rhythms, etc., or accompanied by instruments.

Maestoso (It., măh-ĕ-stŏh´sŏh). Majestic, dignified.

Maestro (It,. măh-ĕh´strŏh). Master. . .*Maestro di cappella,* choirmaster; conductor.

Maggiore. In Italian, major.

Magnificat (L., măhg-nē´fē-kăht). "Magnificat anima mea dominum" (my soul doth magnify the Lord), the canticle of the Virgin Mary (Luke I:46-55) sung as part of the Office of Vespers in the Roman Catholic Church.

Main (Fr., măn). Hand. . . *Main droite,* right hand; *main gauche,* left hand.

Maître (Fr., mä´tr). Master. . . *Maître de chapelle,* choirmaster; conductor.

Majeur. French for major.

Major. "Greater"; opposed to minor, "lesser." See INTERVAL. . . *Major cadence,* one closing on a major triad. . . *M. chord,* one having a major third and perfect fifth.

Major scale. A scale consisting of 2 major seconds, 1 minor second, 3 major seconds, and 1 minor second in this order.

Major second. An interval of 2 semitones.

Major seventh. An interval 1 semitone short of an octave.

Major third. An interval of 2 whole tones.

Malinconico (It., măh-lin-kô´nē-kŏh). Melancholy, dejected.

Mambo. A ballroom dance of West Indian origin similar to the cha-cha and rumba.

Mancando (It., măhn-kăhn´dŏh). Decreasing in loudness, dying away.

Mandola (It., măhn-dô´läh). A large mandolin.

Mandolin. A small kind of lute, the body shaped like half a pear; with wire strings tuned pairwise, played with a plectrum and stopped on a fingerboard.

Mandora, Mandore. Same as MANDOLA.

M

Maniera (It., măh-nē-â′răh). Manner, style, method. . . *Con dolce maniera,* in a suave, delicate style.

Mano (It., mah′nŏh). Hand. . . *Mano destra* (*sinistra*), right (left) hand.

Manual. An organ keyboard; opposed to *pedal.*

Maracas. Latin American rattles, usually in pairs, shaken vigorously.

Marcato, -a (It., mar-kăh′tŏh, -tăh, "marked"). With distinctness and emphasis.

March. A composition of strongly marked rhythm, suitable for timing the steps of a body of persons proceeding at a walking pace.— *March form* is in duple ($\frac{2}{4}$), compound duple ($\frac{6}{8}$), or quadruple ($\frac{4}{4}$) time, with reprises of 4, 8, or 16 measures, followed by a Trio section, and ending with a repetition of the march.

Marcia (It., mar′chăh). March. . . *Alla marcia,* in march style.

Marimba. Xylophone with tuned resonators placed underneath the wooden bars.

Markiert (Ger., mar-keert′). Accented, marked.

Marsch (Ger., marsh). March.

Martellato (It., mar-tel-lah′tŏh). "Hammered"; on the violin, play the notes with a sharp, decided stroke; on the piano, strike the keys with a heavy, inelastic plunge of the finger, or (in octave playing) with the arm staccato.

Marziale (It., mar-tsē-ah′lĕh). Martial, warlike.

Masque. A kind of musical drama, popular in the 16th and 17th centuries; a spectacular play with vocal and instrumental music.

Mass. In the Roman Catholic Church, the musical service taking place during the consecration of the elements, with 5 divisions; (1) Kyrie, (2) Gloria, (3) Credo, (4) Sanctus and Benedictus, (5) Agnus Dei. . . *High Mass,* one celebrated at church festivals, with music and incense. . . *Low Mass,* one without music.

Mässig (Ger., mä′sĭyh). Measured; moderate.

Matins. The music sung at morning prayer; the first of the Canonical Hours.

Mazurka (Polish, măh-zoor′kăh). A Polish national dance in triple time and moderate tempo with a variable accent on the third beat.

M.d. Abbreviation for Main droite or Mano destra.

Me. Stands for Mi, in Tonic Sol-fa.

Measure. 1. The notes and rests comprised between 2 bars; the metrical unit in composition, with regular accentuation, familiarly called a "bar."

Medesimo (It., mĕh-dā′zē-mŏh). The same.

Mediant. The 3rd degree of the scale.

Medley. See POTPOURRI.

Meistersinger (Ger., mī´ster-zing´er). Mastersinger(s); in Germany, the 15th–16th-century artisan successors to the 12th–14th-century aristocratic MINNESINGERS.

Melancolia (It., mā-lăhn-kŏh-lē´ăh). Melancholy.

Mélange (Fr., mā-lahn´zh). A medley, potpourri.

Melisma. A melodic ornament or grace; coloratura.—*Melismatic*, ornamented, embellished; *m. song*, that in which more than one tone is sung to a syllable.

Melodic. 1. In the style of a melody.—2. Vocal, singable; as a melodic interval.

Melodrama. Originally, a musical drama; now (1) stage declamation with a musical accompaniment; (2) a romantic and sensational drama in which music plays a subordinate part.

Melody. 1. The rational progression of single tones; contrasted with harmony, the rational combination of several tones.—2. The leading part.—3. An air or tune.

Melos (Gk., mā´lŏhs, "song"). The name bestowed by Wagner on the style of recitative employed in his later musical dramas.

Même (Fr., mäm). Same. . . *À la même*, tempo primo.

Meno (It., mā´nŏh). Less; not so. . . *Meno allegro*, not so fast.—*Meno* alone stands for *meno mosso*, not so fast.

Mensural notation. Various types of rhythmic notation in use from the 13th to the 17th centuries.

Menuet (Fr., mŭ-nü-ā´). A minuet.

Messa di voce (It., mes´săh dē voh´chĕh). The attack of a sustained vocal tone *pianissimo*, with a swell to *fortissimo*, and slow decrease to *pianissimo* again:

Mesto (It., mĕh´stŏh). Pensive, sad, melancholy.

Mesuré (Fr., mŭ-zü-rā´). 1. Measured, moderate.—2. In exact time.

Meter. 1. In music, the symmetrical grouping of musical rhythms.—2. In verse, the division into symmetrical lines.

Metronome. A double pendulum moved by clockwork, and provided with a slider on a graduated scale marking the number of beats the metronome makes per minute. Modern metronomes are electric and have no pendulum.

Mezzo, -a (It., med´zŏh, -zăh). Half.—Written alone, it refers to the preceding *f* or *p*, thus meaning "mezzo *forte*" or mezzo *piano*". . . *Mezzo legato*, in piano playing, calls for a light touch with less pressure than in legato. . . *Mezza voce*, "with half the power of the voice"; calls for *mezzo forte*, both in singing and playing.

Mezzo-soprano (It., med´zŏh-sŏh-prah´nŏh). The female voice between soprano and alto, partaking of the quality of both, and usually of small compass (*a-f* ² or *g* ²), but very full-toned in the medium register.

M.g. Abbreviation for "main gauche," *left hand* in French.

Mi. The 3rd Aretinian syllable; name of the note *E* in France, Italy, etc.

Middle C. The *C* in the middle of the piano keyboard:

MIDI. An abbreviation for Musical Instrument Digital Interface; it is a digital communications specification that enables electronic instruments, computers, and such equipment to communicate and interact with each other.

Minaccioso (It., mē-nǎht-chŏh´sŏh). In a menacing or threatening manner.

Miniature score. An orchestral score reproduced in a small size so that it can be used for study purposes.

Minim. A half note. . . *Minim rest*, a half rest.

Minnesinger (Ger., min´nĕ-zing´er; *singular and plural*). The German aristocratic poet-musicians of the 12th–14th centuries.

Minor. Latin word for "smaller," used in music in 2 different senses: 1. To indicate a *smaller* interval of a kind, as in minor second, etc.;—2. To define a key, as in *a* minor, or a scale as in *a* minor scale; in minor keys the third of the scale forms an interval of a minor third from the root.

Minor harmonic scale. A minor scale with the raised seventh degree providing a leading tone.

Minor melodic scale. A minor scale that eliminates the interval of an augmented second between the sixth and seventh degrees of the harmonic minor scale, thereby providing a smoother melodic progression. When ascending, the sixth and seventh degrees are raised; when descending, these notes are unaltered.

Minor natural scale. A minor scale without chromatic alterations, and therefore lacking the leading tone.

Minstrels. In the Middle Ages, professional musicians who sang or declaimed poems, often of their own composition, to a simple instrumental accompaniment.

Minuet. An early French dance form. As an art product it is usually a double minuet, the first section repeated after the second (the Trio). It is in triple time.

Miracle play. Sacred dramas, often with music, which were popular in England in the Middle Ages; the stories were usually on biblical subjects or parables.

Mirliton (Fr., meer´lĕ-tŏhn). Same as KAZOO.

Mirror canon. A canon sounding the same when sung or played backwards.

Missa (Latin). The Mass. . . *Missa brevis*, short Mass. . . *solemnis*, high Mass.

Misterioso (It., mē-stĕh-rē-oh´sŏh). Suggesting mystery or hidden meaning.

Misurato (It., mē-zoo-rah´tŏh). With the measure; in exact time.

Mit (Ger., mit). With. . . *Mit Ausdruck*, with expression. . . *Mit Begleitung*, accompanied. . . *Mit halber Stimme*, mezza voce. . . *Mit Kraft*, powerfully.

Mixed cadence. See AUTHENTIC CADENCE. . . *Mixed chorus, quartet, voices,* vocal music combining male and female voices.

Mixolydian mode. A mode corresponding to the progression from *G* to *G* on the white keys of the piano.

Modal harmony. The type of harmony derived from church, exotic, or invented modes, apart from the common major and minor.

Mode. 1. A generic term applied to ancient Greek melodic progressions and to church scales established in the Middle Ages and codified in the system of Gregorian chant. The intervals of the Greek modes were counted downwards, and those of the medieval modes were counted upwards, so the intervallic contents were different between the Greek and the church systems. However, the church modes retained the Greek names of the modes. See IONIAN; DORIAN; PHRYGIAN; LYDIAN; MIXOLYDIAN; AEOLIAN; AND LOCRIAN.—2. The distinction between a major key (mode) and minor key (mode).—3. Any scalar pattern of intervals, either traditional or invented.—4. A system of 13th-century rhythmic notation.

Moderato (It., mŏh-dĕh-rah´tŏh). Moderate; that is, at a moderate tempo, or rate of speed. . . *Allegro moderato*, moderately fast.

Modulate. To pass from one key or mode into another.

Modulation. Passage from one key or mode into another. . . *Chromatic modulation*, one effected by use of diatonic intervals. . . *Diatonic mod.*, one effected by use of diatonic intervals. . . *Enharmonic mod.*, one effected by using enharmonic changes to alter the significance of tones or intervals. . . *Final mod.*, one in which the new key is retained, or still another follows. . . *Passing, Transient, Transitory mod.*, one in which the original key is speedily regained.

Möglich (Ger., mö´glĭyh). Possible. . . *So rasch wie möglich*, as fast as possible.

Moll (Ger., mōhl). Minor.

Molto, -a (It., mōhl´tŏh, -täh). Very, much. . . *Molto adagio*, very slowly. . . *Molto allegro*, very fast. . . *Con molta passione*, with great passion. . . *Di molto* or *Molto molto*, exceedingly, extremely.

Monochord. An ancient musical instrument having a single string, which was stretched over a soundbox and a shifting bridge that allowed the string to be adjusted to different pitches.

Monodrama. A dramatic or musical presentation, with a single performer.

72

Monody. The recitative-like accompanied song style of early 17th-century Italy.

Monophony. Unaccompanied melody.

Monothematic. A composition with a single subject.

Monotone. 1. A single unaccompanied and unvaried tone.—2. Recitation (intoning, chanting) on such a tone.

Morbido (It., môr′bē-dŏh). Soft, tender.

Morceau (Fr., mor-sōh′). A piece, composition.

Mordent. A grace consisting of the single rapid alternation of a principal note with an auxiliary a minor second below:

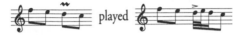

Inverted mordent, the alternation of the principal note with the higher auxiliary:

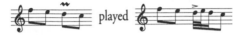

Morendo (It., mŏh-ren′dŏh). Dying away.

Moresca (It., mŏh-rĕs′căh). A Moorish dance.

Mormoroso (It., mor-mŏh-roh′sŏh). Murmuring; in a very gentle, subdued tone.

Morris dance. An old English dance often in the form of a symbolic character play.

Mosso (It., môhs′sŏh). "Moved." Standing alone, as a tempo mark, it is the same as "*con moto.*" It means "rapid" in the phrases *meno mosso* (less rapid), *più mosso* (more rapid), and *poco mosso* (somewhat rapid). . . *Allegretto poco mosso,* a rather lively allegretto, almost allegro. . . *Mosso agitato,* a fast and agitated movement; *assai mosso e agitato,* very rapid and agitated.

Motet. A contrapuntal sacred vocal composition without accompaniment.

Motif (Fr., mŏh-tēf′). Motive.

Motion. 1. The progression of a single part or melody; it is *conjunct* when progressing by steps, *disjunct* when progressing by skips.— 2. The movement of one part in relation to another; in *contrary* or *opposite* motion one part ascends while the other descends; in *oblique* motion one part retains its tone while the other moves; in *parallel* motion, both parts move up or down by the same interval; in *similar* motion both move together by dissimilar intervals; in mixed motion, two or more of the above varieties occur at once between several parts.

Moto (It., mô′tŏh). Motion; speed; movement, tempo.—*Con moto,* with an animated and energetic movement. . . *Moto precedente,* at the former tempo. . . *Più (meno) moto,* same as *più (meno) mosso.*

Moto perpetuo. "Perpetual motion"; applied to short, fast pieces in rondo form.

Mouth organ. A harmonica.

Mouthpiece. That part of a wind instrument which a player places upon or between the lips.

Movable Doh. A system of solfeggio in which the tonic of every major scale is called Doh, the 2nd degree called Re, etc.

Movement. 1. Tempo.—2. A principal division or section of a composition.

Movendo il tempo (It., mŏh-ven´dŏh ēl tem´pŏh). Growing faster.

M.s. Abbreviation for "mano sinistra," *left hand* in Italian.

Munter (Ger., mŏŏn´ter). Lively, gay, animated.

Musette (Fr., mü-zet´). A kind of bagpipe; also, a short piece imitating this bagpipe, with a drone bass.

Music box. The Swiss music box has a metal cylinder or barrel, studded with pins, and turned by clockwork; in revolving, the pins catch and twang a comblike row of steel teeth, each tooth producing a tone.

Music drama. The original description of opera as it evolved in Florence early in the 17th century; Wagner adopted this term in order to emphasize the dramatic element in his spectacles.

Musica (It., moo´zē-kăh). Music. . . *Dramma per musica,* an opera.

Musica ficta (L., moo´zē-kă fĭk´tah). In music from the 10th through the 16th centuries, chromatic alterations conjectured to have been made in performance.

Musica figurata (It., — fĭ-gyoor-a´tah). Music arranged in contrasting contrapuntal figurations.

Musica reservata (L., — rĕ-zer-văh´tah). A 16th-century term applied to a particularly sophisticated type of contrapuntal music, related to musica ficta and "reserved" for masters of the craft.

Musical saw. Quasi-musical instrument producing a twanging sound when stroked.

Musicology. The science of music. The concept includes all branches of music—theory, history, aesthetics, lexicography, bibliography, etc.

Musique (Fr., mü-zēk´). Music.

Musique concrète (Fr., —con-crĕt´). "Concrete music"; a practice in which all kinds of sounds and noises are used, similar to collage technique in modern art.

Muta (It., moo´tăh). "Change!" (crook or instrument).

Mutation. 1. Change of voice.—2. Change of position, shifting (violin).

Mute. 1. A heavy piece of metal fitted to the bridge of a violin, etc., to deaden the sound. The direction for putting on the mutes is "con sordini"; for taking them off, "senza sordini."—2. A leather-covered pad, pasteboard cone, or wooden cylinder inserted in the bell of the horn or trumpet to modify the tone.

Mut(h)ig (Ger., moo′tǐyh). Spiritedly, boldly.

Mysteries. Medieval Bible plays, often with vocal and instrumental music.

N

Nach (Ger., năh). After; according to.

Nachahmung (Ger., —äh´mŭng^k). Imitation.

Nachdrücklich (Ger., —drŭk´lĭyh). With emphasis, strongly marked.

Nachlassend (Ger., —läh´sent). Yieldingly, slower and slower; *rallentando.*

Nachlässig (Ger., —les´sĭyh). Carelessly.

Nachschlag (Ger., —shläyh). The end notes of a trill.

Nachtmusik ger., năht´-moo-zĭk). Night music, a serenade.

Nachstück (Ger., năht´shtŭk). "Night piece," a nocturne.

Nach und nach (Ger., năh ŏŏnt năh´). Little by little, gradually.

Natural. 1. The sign ♮.—2. A white key on the keyboard. . . *Natural harmonics*, those produced on an open string. . . *Natural horn*, the French horn without valves. . . *Natural pitch*, that of any wind instrument when not overblown. . . *Natural tone*, any tone obtained on a wind instrument with cupped mouthpiece, without using keys, valves, or the slide.

Neapolitan sixth. The first inversion of a flat two chord (♭II); in *C* major, the notes *F, A♭, D♭,*

Negli (It., näl´yē). In the.

Nei, nell', nella, nelle, nello (It.). In the.

Nervoso (It., nâr-voh´sŏh). In a forcible, agitated style.

Netto, -a (It., net´tŏh, -tăh). In a neat, clear, distinct style.

Neumes. Signs used, in the early Middle Ages, to represent tones.

Nicht (Ger., nĭyht). Not. . . *Nicht zu langsam*, not too slow.

Niente (It., nē-en´tĕh). Nothing. . . *Quasi niente*, barely audible.

Ninth. The interval of an octave, plus a major or minor Second.

Nobilmente (It., nŏh-bēl-men´tĕh). In a refined, chaste, lofty style.

Noch (Ger., nŏh). Still; yet. . . *Noch rascher*, still faster.

Nocturne (Fr., nŏhk-tū rn´). A piece of a dreamily romantic or sentimental character, without fixed form.

Nocturns. Services of the Church held during the night.

Node. A point or line in a vibrating body (such as a string, soundboard, trumpet, bell) that remains at rest during the vibration of the other parts of the body.

Noël (Fr., nōĕl). A Christmas carol or hymn.

Noire (Fr., nwăhr). Quarter note.

Non (It. nŏhn). Not.

Nonet. A composition for nine voices or instruments.

Nota cambiata. An extra note inserted one diatonic degree above the principal note before descending to the next note (as the note *D* inserted between *C* and *B*).

Notation. The art of representing musical tones, and their modifications, by means of written characters.

Note. One of the signs used to express the relative time value of tones. . . *Note against note*, counterpoint in equal notes.

Notturno (It., nŏht-toor´nŏh). A Nocturne.

Novellette (Ger., nŏh-vel-let´tĕ). An instrumental piece in form, bold in harmony, and romantic in character.

Nuance (Fr., nü-ahnss´). Shading; change in musical expression, either in the tone color, tempo, or degree of force.

Number. 1. A subdivision of an opera or oratorio.—2. A smaller portion of a large work, such as a song, aria, interlude, etc.—3. Any single piece on a program.—4. An opus number.

Nuovamente (It., nŏŏ-ŏh-văh-men´tĕh). Again, anew.

Nut. 1. The ridge over which the strings pass at the end of the fingerboard next to the head of a violin, etc.—2. The sliding projection at the lower end of the violin bow, by means of which the hair is tightened or slackened.—3. The "lower nut" on the violin is the ridge between the tailpiece and tailpin (or button).

O

O. A small circle signifies *(a)* an open string. *(b)* the harmonic mark; *(c)* the diminished fifth.

O (It., ŏh). Or. (Written before either vowels or consonants; *od* is an unusual form.)

Obbligato (It., ŏhb-blē-gah′tŏh). Required, indispensable. An *obbligato* part is a concerted instrumental part; especially when accompanying a vocal solo.

Oblique motion. A type of 2-part counterpoint in which one voice moves and the other remains stationary.

Oboe. An orchestral instrument with conical wooden tube, 9 to 14 keys, and a double reed; compass 2 octaves and a Seventh from *b*♭ to *a*³. Tone very reedy and penetrating, though mild.

Oboe da caccia (It., oh′boh-eh dăh căh′tchăh). Literally, "oboe of the hunt." An instrument tuned a fifth below the oboe; in use during the Renaissance.

Oboe d'amore (It., —dăh-moh′reh). Literally, "oboe of love." An oboe that sounds a minor third below the written notation.

Ocarina (It., ô-kăh-rē′năh). "Goose-pipe"; a bird-shaped wind instrument of terra cotta, with finger holes and a whistle mouthpiece.

Octave. 1. A series of 8 consecutive diatonic tones.—2. The interval between the 1st and 8th tones of such a series... *Concealed, covered,* or *hidden octaves* (or *fifths*), parallel octaves (or fifths) suggested by the progression of 2 parts in similar motion to the interval of an octave (or fifth)... *Rule of the octave,* a series of harmonies written over the diatonic scale as a bass.

Octet. A composition for 8 voices or instruments.

Octuor (Fr., ŏhk-tü-ohr′). An octet.

Ode. A chorus in ancient Greek plays; a musical work of praise.

Oder (Ger., oh′der). Or; or else.

Offertorium (L., ô-führ-tō′rē-ŭm). Offertory; in the Roman Catholic Mass, the verses or anthem following the Credo, and sung by the choir while the priest is placing the consecrated elements on the altar, during which the offerings of the congregation are collected.

Ohne (Ger., oh′ně). Without.

Oliphant. An ancient hunting horn, sometimes made of elephant's tusk.

Omnitonic. Having or producing all tones; chromatic (instrument).

Ondeggiamento (It., ŏhn-ded-jăh-men′tŏh). Undulation; rocking (as by waves).

Ondulé (Fr.). Undulated, wavy.

Ongarese (It.). Hungarian.

Open harmony. In 4-part harmony, an arrangement of voices such that the 3 upper voices have a total range of more than an octave (as in C, G, E, C).

Open pedal. The loud piano pedal.

Open string. A string on the violin, viola, or cello sounding its natural tone without being stopped by the finger.

Opera. A form of drama in which music is essential and predominant. The several acts, usually preceded by instrumental introductions, consist of vocal scenes, recitatives, songs, arias, duets, trios, choruses, etc., accompanied by the orchestra. This is *Grand* or *Heroic opera; Comic opera* has spoken interludes.

Opera buffa (It., ôh′pā-răh bŏŏf′făh). Light comic opera.

Opéra comique (Fr., ŏh-pā-răh kŏh-mēk′). French opera with spoken dialogue instead of recitative. It is not necessarily comic in nature.

Opera seria (It., ôh′pā-răh sā′rē-ăh). Serious (grand, heroic, tragic) opera.

Operetta. A "little opera"; the libretto is in a comic, mock-pathetic, parodistic, or anything but serious vein; music light and lively, often interrupted by dialogue.

Ophicleide (ŏf′ĭ-klīd). The bass instrument of the key bugle family.

Opposite motion. Contary motion.

Opus (Latin). Work; often written *Op.*, or *op.*

Oratorio (It., ŏh-răh-tô′rē-ŏh). An extended composition for vocal solos and chorus, with orchestral or organ accompaniment and sung without staging or scenery.

Orchestra (or′kĕs-trăh). A group of musicians performing on the instruments employed in opera, oratorio, or symphony; hence, the instruments, taken together.

Orchestral (or-kĕs′tral, or or′kĕs-tral). Pertaining to, or resembling, the orchestra.

Orchestration. The art of writing music for orchestral performance; the science of combining, in an effective manner, the instruments constituting the orchestra.

Organ. A keyboard wind instrument consisting of sets of pipes played from one or more keyboards; there may be 5 keyboards for the fingers (manuals), and usually 1 for the feet (pedal, or pedal keyboard). The pipes, of which there are two main divisions, flue pipes and reed pipes, are arranged in sets (registers, or stops), and made to speak by wind admitted from the bellows on pressing the keys.

Organ point. A tone sustained in one part to harmonies executed in the other parts, usually a bass tone, tonic or dominant (or both).

Organum (L., ôr´găn-ŭm). The earliest attempts at harmonic or polyphonic music, in which 2 parts progressed in parallel fifths and fourths.

Orgel (Ger., ohr´gel); **Orgue** (Fr., ohrg). Organ.

Ornament. A grace, embellishment.

Osservato (It., ŏhs-sâr-vah´tŏh). Carefully observed; *stile osservato*, strict style.

Ossia (It., ŏhs-sē´äh). Or; or else; indicates an alternative (or facilitated) reading or fingering of a passage. (Also *Oppure, Ovvero*.)

Ostinato (It., ŏh-stē-nah´tŏh). "Obstinate"; the incessant repetition of a theme with a varying contrapuntal accompaniment. . . *Basso ostinato*, ground bass.

Ottava (It., ŏht-tah´văh). Octave. . . *All'octava* (written 8va----- or 8------, "at the octave," an octave higher. . . *Coll'ottava*, "with the octave," that is, in octaves. . . *Ottava alta*, the higher octave. . . *Ottava bassa* (8va *bassa*), the lower octave, an octave below.

Ottavino. A piccolo.

Ottoni. In Italian, brass instruments.

Ottetto (It. ŏht-tet´tŏh). An octet.

Ou (Fr., oo). Or; or else.

Overblow. With wind instruments, to force the wind through the tube in such a way as to cause any harmonic to sound.

Overstring. To arrange the strings of a piano in 2 sets, one lying over and diagonally crossing the other; a piano so strung is called an *overstrung* piano.

Overtone. Harmonic tone.

Overture. A musical introduction to an opera, oratorio, etc.—A concert overture is an independent composition in sonata form.

Ovvero (It. ŏhv-vâh´roh). Or; or else.

P

P. Stands for *Pedal* (P. *or Ped.*); *piano* (**p**), **pp** or **ppp**, *pianissimo*; *P.F.*, pianoforte; **pf**, pianoforte (soft, increasing to loud); **fp**, forte piano (loud, diminishing to soft instantly); **mp**, mezzo piano (half soft); *Pointe* (Fr., "toe").

Pandiatonicism. A modern term for a system of diatonic harmony making use of all 7 degrees of the scale in dissonant combinations, as for instance in the concluding chord *C, G, E, A, D, G.*

Panpipes. A set of different-sized pipes bundled together and blown across the top.

Pantomime. A ballet-like performance without speech or singing, in which the action is suggested by gestures and choreography.

Parallel motion. Voice-leading in harmony or counterpoint in which intervals move in the same direction. In traditional harmony parallel thirds and sixths are recommended, but parallel fifths and octaves are forbidden.

Paraphrase. A transcription or rearrangement of a vocal or instrumental piece for some other instrument or instruments, with variations.

Parlando (It., par-lăhn´dŏh), **Parlante** (It., par-lăhn´těh). "Speaking"; singing with clear and marked enunciation.—In piano playing, a clear, crisp *non legato*.

Parody. As used in music theory, this term means "like something else," and was quite devoid of the contemporary sense of travesty. A *parody Mass* is a work with thematic material taken from a work by another composer.

Part. 1. The series of tones written for and executed by a voice or instrument, either as a solo or together with other voices or instruments.—2. A division of a homophonic movement devoted to the exposition of one melody, or musical idea; like the 2-part and 3-part song forms.

Partial tone. A harmonic tone.

Partita (It., par-tē´tăh). A suite.

Partition (Fr., păr-tē-sĭ-ohn´), **Partitur** (Ger., păr-tē-toor). A score.

Part music. Concerted or harmonized vocal music.

Part song. A composition for at least 3 voices in harmony, without accompaniment, and for equal or mixed voices. It is properly a melody with choral harmony, with any reasonable number of voices to each part.

Passacaglia (It., păhs-săh-cahl´yăh). An old Italian dance in triple time and stately movement, written on a ground bass of 4 measures.

Passacaille (Fr., păh-săh-cah´ē). Passacaglia.

Passage. 1. A portion or secton of a piece, usually short.—2. A rapid repeated figure, either ascending or descending. A scale passage is generally called a run.

Passamezzo (It., păhs-săh-měd´zŏh). An old Italian dance in duple time.

Passepied (Fr., păhs-p'yā). An old French dance in ⅜ or ⅚ time, with 3 or 4 reprises; like the minuet in movement, but quicker.

Passing tones. Notes foreign to the chords that they accompany, and passing by a step from one chord to another. They differ from suspensions in not being prepared, and in entering (usually) on an unaccented beat.

Passion. A musical setting of a text describing Christ's sufferings and death.

Pasticcio (It., păhs-tit´chŏh), **Pastiche** (Fr., păhs-tēsh´). A musical medley of extracts from different works, pieced together and provided with new words so as to form a "new" composition.

Pastoral(e). 1. A scenic cantata or opera representing pastoral life.—2. An instrumental piece imitating in style and instrumentation rural and idyllic scenes.

Pauken (Ger., pow´ken). Timpani.

Pausa (It., pah´ŏŏ-zăh). A rest; a pause. . . *Pausa lunga,* long pause; *pause generale,* pause for all performers.

Pavan(e). A stately dance of Italian or Spanish origin, in slow tempo and ⅔ time.

Ped. Stands for *Pedal;* signifies that the right (loud) piano pedal is to be pressed; or (in organ music) that notes so marked are to be played on the pedals.

Pedal. 1. A foot key on the organ or pedal piano.—2. A foot lever; as the piano pedals, or the organ swell-pedal.

Pedal organ. The set of stops controlled by the organ pedals.

Pedal point. An organ point.

Pedal tone. A sustained or continuously repeated tone.

Pensiero (It., pen-sē-â´roh). A thought. . . *Pensiero del(la)—,* Recollections of—.

Pentatonic scale. A 5-tone scale, usually that which avoids semitonic steps by skipping the 4th and 7th degrees in major, and the 2nd and 6th in minor.

Per (It., pĕr). For, by, from, in, through.

Percussion. 1. The striking or sounding of a dissonance.—2. The striking of one body against another.

Perdendosi (It., pâr-den´dŏh-sē). Dying away.

Perfect cadence. One consisting of the dominant triad followed by the tonic triad.

Perfect intervals. The standard octave, fifth, and fourth.

Perfect pitch. ABSOLUTE PITCH.

Period. A complete musical thought of 8 (12) or 16 measures, ending with an authentic CADENCE.

Perpetual canon. A canon in which the final cadence leads back into the opening measures, like a round.

Pesante (It., pěh-sähn′těh). Heavy, ponderous; firm, vigorous.

Peu à peu (Fr., pö äh pö′). Little by little. . . *Un peu,* a little.

Pezzo (It., pet′sŏh). A piece; a number (of an opera, etc.)

Phantasiestück (Ger., fähn-tăh-zē′sht*ü*k). A fantasia.

Phrase. Half of an 8-measure period.—Also, any short figure or passage complete in itself and unbroken in continuity.

Phrase mark. A curved line connecting the notes of a phrase.

Phrasing. 1. The bringing out into proper relief of the phrases.—2. The signs of notation devised to further the above end.

Phrygian mode. A church MODE corresponding to the scale from *E* to *E* on the white keys of the piano.

Piacevole (It., p′yăh-chā′vŏh-lěh). Pleasant, agreeable; calls for a smooth, suave delivery, free from strong accents.

Piangevole (It., p′yăhn-jā′vŏh-lěh). "Weeping"; in a mournful, plaintive style.

Pianino (It., pē-ăh-nē′nŏh). An upright piano.

Pianissimo (It., pē-ăh-nēs′sē-moh). Very soft; abbreviated *p.*

Pianississimo (It., pē-ăh-nēs-sēs′sē-moh). Very, very soft; abbreviated *ppp.*

Piano. 1. Soft, softly (sign *p*). . . *Piano pedal,* the soft or left pedal of the piano.—2. A keyboard string instrument of percussion, the tones being produced by hammers striking the strings. The principal parts are the *Frame,* the *Soundboard,* the *Strings,* the *Action,* and the *Pedals.* The hammer action was first practically developed by Bartolomeo Cristofori of Padua in 1711.

Pianola. Trade name for the player piano.

Piano quartet. Composition for piano, violin, viola, and cello.

Piano quintet. Composition with piano and string quartet.

Piano score. An arrangement of an orchestral work for piano.

Piano trio. A composition for piano, violin, and cello.

Piatti (It., p′yăht′tē). Cymbals.

Pibroch (pē′brŏh). Variations for the bagpipe.

Picardy third. The frequent practice in Baroque music of ending a piece in a minor key with the parallel major tonic chord.

Picchettato (It., pik-ket-tah´tŏh). See Piqué.

Piccolo (It., pik´kŏh-lŏh, "little"). The octave flute; a small flute pitched an octave higher than the orchestral flute.

Pick. To pluck or twang the strings of a guitar, mandolin, etc.— Also, a plectrum.

Pietoso (It., pē-ĕh-toh´sŏh). "Pitiful(ly), moving(ly)"; demands a sympathetic and expressive delivery.

Piffero (It., pif´fĕh-rŏh). 1. A fife; also, a primitive kind of oboe or shawm.

Pincé (Fr., păn-sā´). 1. Plucked; as the strings of the harp.—2. Pizzicato.

Pipe. 1. tubular wind instrument.—2. An organ pipe.

Piqué (Fr., pē-kā´). In violin playing, the mezzo-staccato called for by a slur with staccato dots; notes so marked to be played in one bow (*picchiettato*).

Piston. See Valve.

Pitch. The position of a tone in the musical scale. Pitch is relative, or absolute. The *relative* pitch of a tone is its position (higher or lower) as compared with some other tone. (See Interval). Its *absolute* pitch is its fixed position in the entire range of musical tones. The number of vibrations made by a tone establishes its absolute pitch.

Pitch pipe. A small wooden or metal reed pipe which sounds one or more tones of fixed pitch, to give the tone for tuning an instrument, or for a choir.

Più (It., pew). More.—When *più* stands alone, as a *tempo* mark, *mosso* is implied; as an *expression* mark, it refers to the next preceding *f* or *p*... *Più mosso, più moto*, faster... *Più mosso ancora*, still faster.

Pivot chord. In modulation, a chord pivotal to both the old and the new keys.

Pizzicato (It., pit-sē-kah´tŏh). "Pinched"; plucked with the finger; a direction, in music for bowed instruments, to play the notes by plucking the strings.

Plagal cadence. A cadence in which the final keynote is a fourth above the lowest tone of the mode.

Plainchant, Plainsong. The unison vocal music of the Christian church, probably dating from the first centuries of the Christian era.

Player piano. A mechanical piano in which the keyboard action is produced by a rotating perforated roll.

Plectrum. A pick; a small piece of ivory, tortoise shell, or metal, held between the forefinger and thumb, or fitted to the thumb by a ring, and used to pluck or twang the strings of the mandolin, zither, etc.

Plein (Fr., plăn). Full.

Plus (Fr., plü). More.

Pochissimo (It., poh-kee′cee-moh). Very little.

Poco (It., pô′kōh). Little. . . *A poco a poco*, little by little. . . *Poco allegro*, rather fast. . . *Poco largo*, rather slow.

Poi (It., pô′ē). Then, thereafter.

Pointe (Fr., pwăn′t). 1. Point or head of a bow.—2. Toe (abbrev. *p*).

Polka (pôl′kăh). A lively round dance in $\frac{2}{4}$ time, of Bohemian origin.

Polonaise (Fr., pŏh-lŏh-năz′). A dance of Polish origin, in $\frac{3}{4}$ time and moderate tempo; formerly in animated processional style, but now merely a slow promenade opening a ball.

Polyphonic. 1. Consisting of 2 or more independently treated melodies; contrapuntal.—2. Capable of producing 2 or more tones simultaneously.

Polyphony. The combination in harmonious progression of 2 or more independent melodies; the independent treatment of the parts; counterpoint.

Polytonality. Simultaneous use of two or more different tonalities or keys.

Ponticello (It., pŏhn-tē-chel′lŏh). Bridge.—*Sul ponticello*, near the bridge.

Portamento (It., por-tăh-men′tŏh). A smooth gliding from one tone to another, differing from the legato in its more deliberate execution, and in the actual (though very rapid and slurring) sounding of the intermediate tones.

Portative. A small portable organ which could be used in religious processions.

Posato (It., pŏh-sah′tŏh). Sedate, dignified.

Posaune (Ger., pŏh-zow′nĕ). Trombone.

Positif (Fr., pah-zē-tēf). Choir organ.

Position. 1. The place of the left hand on the fingerboard of the violin, etc.—2. The arrangement of notes in a chord, with reference to the lowest part.—3. Close (open) position, see HARMONY, *close* and *open*.

Possibile (It., pŏhs-sē′bē-lĕh). Possible; *pianissimo possibile*, as soft as possible.

Post horn. A horn without valves or keys, used on post coaches.

Postlude. A closing voluntary on the organ.

Potpourri (Fr., pŏh-pŏŏ-rē´). A musical medley, all kinds of tunes, or parts of tunes, being connected in an arbitary manner.

Poussé (Fr., pŏŏs-sā´). Up-bow.

pp. Pianissimo.

ppp. Planississimo.

Prächtig (Ger., prĕyh´tĭyh). Grandly, majestically.

Pralltriller (Ger., prähl´trĭl-er). Upper mordent.

Precedente (It., prĕh-chĕh-den´tĕh). Preceding. . . *Moto precedente*, in the preceding tempo.

Precentor. A director and manager of a church choir.

Precipitato (It., prĕh-chē-pē-tah´tŏh). With precipitation, impetuosity, dash.

Preciso (It., prĕh-chē´zŏh). With precision.

Prelude. A musical introduction to a composition or drama.

Preparation. The preparation of a dissonance consists in the presence, in the preceding chord and same part, of the tone forming the dissonance.

Prepared piano. A 20th-century practice initiated by the American composer John Cage, in which the timbre of the piano is altered by placing such objects as screws, bolts, and clips on the strings of the grand piano.

Pressante (It. pres-săhn´tĕh). Pressing on, accelerating.

Prestissimo (It., prĕh-stis´sē-mŏh). Very rapidly.

Presto (It., prâ´stŏh). Fast, rapid; faster than *allegro*. . . *Presto assai*, very rapid.

Primary accent. The downbeat; the accent beginning the measure.

Primary triad. One of the 3 fundamental triads of a key (those on the 1st, 5th, and 4th degrees).

Prime. The first note of a scale.

Primo, -a (It., prē´mŏh, -măh). First. . . *Prima donna*, leading lady in opera. . . *Prima vista*, at first sight. . . *Prima volta*, the first time; indicates that the measures under its brackets are to be played the first time, before the repeat; on repeating, those marked *Seconda volta* are to be performed instead.

Principal chords. The basic chords of a key—the triads on the tonic, dominant, and subdominant, with the dominant seventh chord.

Principio (It., prin-chē´pē-ŏh). Beginning, first time. . . *In principio*, at the beginning. . . *Più marcato del principio*, more marked than the first time.

Processional. A hymn sung in church during the entrance of choir and clergy.

Program music. A class of instrumental compositions intended to represent distinct moods or phases of emotion, or to depict actual scenes of events.

Progression. The advance from one tone to another, or from one chord to another; the former is *melodic*, the latter *harmonic* progression.

Pronto (It., prŏhn´tŏh). Promptly, swiftly.

Pronunziato (It., prŏh-nŏŏn-tsē-ah´tŏh). Pronounced, marked; *ben pronunziato*, clearly enunciated.

Proportion. A term of medieval music theory, relating to the proportionate duration of the notes of the melody, and also the ratio of vibrations of these notes.

Psalm. A hymn; a sacred song.

Psaltery (sôl´ter-ĭ). An ancient kind of harp-zither, with a varying number of strings plucked by the fingers or with a plectrum.

Psaume (Fr., sohm). Psalm.

Pulse. A beat or accent.

Pult (Ger., poolt). Music stand.

Punta. (It., pŏŏn´tăh). Point (of the bow). . . *Colla punta dell'arco*, at the point of the bow.

Pupitre (Fr., pü´pē tr). Music stand.

Q

Quadrille (kwŏ-drĭl′). A square dance consisting of 5 (or 6) figures; the time alternates between $\frac{3}{8}$ ($\frac{6}{8}$) and $\frac{2}{4}$.

Quadruple counterpoint. See COUNTERPOINT.

Quadruplet. A group of 4 equal naotes to be executed in the time of 3 or 6 of the same kind in the regular rhythm; written:

Quarter note. A note one-quarter the value of a whole note (♩).

Quarter rest. A rest equal in time value to a quarter note (𝄽).

Quarter tone. Half a semitone.

Quartet. 1. A composition for 4 performers.—2. Also, the performers as a group.

Quasi (It., kwah′zē). As if; nearly; approaching. . . *Andante quasi allegretto*, andante approaching allegretto.

Quatre (Fr., kăh′tr), **Quattro** (It., kwăht′trŏh). Four.

Quatuor (Fr., kwăh-tü-or′). A quartet.

Quaver. British term for an eighth note.

Quickstep. A march, usually in $\frac{6}{8}$ time.

Quintet. 1. A composition for 5 performers.—2. Also, the performers as a group.

Quintuor (Fr., kăn-tü-or′). A quintet.

Quintuple rhythm, time. Has 5 beats to the measure.

Quintuplet. A group of 5 equal notes to be executed in the time of 4 of the same kind in the regular rhythm; written:

Quodlibet. A piece employing several well-known tunes from various sources, performed either simultaneously or in succession; a musical medley; potpourri.

R

R. Stands for right (Ger., *rechte*); *r.h.* right hand (*rechte Hand*).

Rabbia, con (It., kŏhn răhb´bē-ăh). With passion, frenzy; furiously.

Raddolcito (It., răhd-dŏhl-chē´tŏh). Gentler, calmer.

Raga. A generic term for a Hindu scale, consisting of 5-7 tones and calculated to create a certain mood. Each raga is suited to a particular time of day.

Ragtime. A syncopated American music of black origins, popular from about 1896 to 1918.

Rallentando (It., răhl-len-tăhn´dŏh). Growing slower and slower.

Rank. A row of organ pipes.

Rasch (Ger., răhsh). Fast, rapid, swift. . . *Noch rascher*, still faster.

Ravvivando il tempo (It., răhv-vē-văhn´dŏh). Accelerating the tempo.

Ray. Stands for RE, in Tonic Sol-fa.

Re (It., ră), **Ré** (Fr., ră). Second of the Aretinian syllables, and the name of the note *D* in France, Italy, etc.

Rebec. A medieval violin, shaped like a half pear, with 3 gut strings.

Recapitulation. A return of the initial section of a movement in sonata form.

Recessional. A hymn sung in church during the departure of choir and clergy after a service.

Recht (Ger., rĕyht). Right; *rechte Hand*, right hand.

Recital. A concert at which either *(a)* all the pieces are executed by one performer, or *(b)* all pieces performed are by one composer.

Recitative (rĕs´ĭ-ta-tēv´). 1. Declamatory singing, free in tempo and rhythm.—2. In piano playing, a crisp delivery of the melody, free in tempo and rhythm.

Reciting note. The tone on which most of each verse in a chant (psalm or canticle) is continuously recited; the dominant.

Recorder. Type of flute of the end-blown variety with a whistle mouthpiece.

Reduction. Rearrangement of a composition for a smaller number of instruments, while preserving its form as far as possible.

Reed. A thin strip of cane, wood, or metal, so adjusted before an aperture as nearly to close it, fixed at one end, and set by an air current in vibration, which it communicates either to an enclosed column of air (organ pipe, oboe), or directly to the free atmosphere, thus producing a musical tone. A *Free reed* vibrates within the aperture without striking the edges; a *Beating reed* strikes on the edges. A *Double reed* is two beating reeds which strike against each other.

Reed instrument. One whose tone is produced by the vibration of a reed in its mouthpiece.

Reed organ. A keyboard instrument whose tones are produced by free reeds.

Reed pipe. See Pipe.

Reel. A lively dance of Scotland and Ireland, usually in $\frac{4}{4}$ (sometimes $\frac{6}{4}$) time, with reprises of 8 measures; danced by 2 couples.

Refrain. A recurring melody of a song, usually at the end of a stanza; in popular music, a chorus.

Regal. A portable organ with reed pipes used during the 16th and 17th centuries.

Reggae. Jamaican popular music, marked by insistent square rhythms.

Register. 1. A set of pipes or reeds controlled by one draw-stop; an organ stop. —2. A portion of the vocal compass; as *high, low, chest,* or *head* register.—3. A portion in an instrument's range differing in quality from other portions.

Registration. 1. The art of effectively employing and combining the various stops of the organ.—2. The combinations of stops employed for any given composition.

Relation(ship). The degree of affinity between keys, chords, and tones.

Relative key. A minor key is relative to that major key, the tonic of which lies a minor Third above its own; a major key is relative to that minor key, the tonic of which lies a minor Third below its own.

Relative pitch. Ability to name an interval or pitch after hearing a given note.

Remote key. An unrelated key.

Renaissance. In music history, the period from 1400 to 1600.

Repeat. 1. The sign ▐▐ or ▐▐ or ▐▐ , *a* signifying that the music between the double-dotted bars is to be repeated; *b* and *c*, that the preceding and also the following division is to be repeated.—2. A section or division of music which is repeated.

Répétiteur (Fr., rĕh-pĕh-tē-tŭhr′). A choral assistant; one who conducts rehearsal.

Répétition (Fr., rĕh-pĕh-tē-sē-on′). A rehearsal.

Reprise (Fr., rŭ-prĕz′). 1. A Repeat 2.—2. The revival of a work.— 3. Reentrance of a part or theme after a rest or pause.

Requiem. The first word in the Mass for the dead; hence, the title of the musical setting of that Mass.

Resolution. The progression of a dissonance to a consonance. *Direct resolution* is immediate progression from the dissonance to the consonance; *Indirect* (or *delayed, deferred, retarded*) *resolution* passes through some intermediate dissonance or dissonances before reaching the final restful consonance.

Response. 1. Responsory.—2. Answer.—3. The musical reply, by the choir or congregation, to what is said or sung by the priest or officiant.

Responsory. 1. That psalm, or part of one, sung between the missal lessons.—2. The Gradual.—3. A Respond; that is, a part of a psalm (formerly an entire psalm) sung between the lessons at the canonical hours.

Rest. A pause or interval of silence between two tones; hence, the sign indicating such a pause.

Restez (Fr., res-tā′). "Stay there!" In music for bowed instruments this direction means *(a)* "Play on the same string," or *(b)* "Remain in the same position (shift)."

Retardation. A holding back, decreasing in speed.

Retenu. French for RITENUTO, holding back.

Retrograde. Performing a melody backwards; a crab movement.

Reveille. The military signal for rising.

Reverse motion. Contrary motion.

Reversion. Retrograde imitation.

Rhythm. The measured movement of similar tone groups; that is, the effect produced by systematic grouping of tones with reference to regularity both in accentuation and in their succession as equal or unequal in time value. *A Rhythm* is, therefore, a tone group serving as a pattern for succeeding identical groups.

Rhythm and blues. A type of black, urban, popular music combining the elements of strong repetitive rhythms, simple melodies and harmonies and blues.

Rhythm section. Percussion section in a jazz band consisting of piano, bass, and drums, supplying the main beat.

Ribs. The curved sides of the violin, connecting belly and back.

Ricercare (It., rē-châr-kăh′rĕh). Instrumental composition of the 16th and 17th centuries generally characterized by imitative treatment of the theme or themes.

Riddle canon. A canon that is not written out so that the performer must find out when the imitating voices must come in.

Rilasciando (It., rē-läh-shăhn′dŏh). RALLENTANDO.

Rinforzato (It., rin-for-tsah′tŏh). With special emphasis; indicates a sudden increase in loudness, either for a tone or chord, or throughout a phrase or short passage.

Ripetizione (It., rē-pĕh-tē-tsē-oh′nĕh). Repetition.

Ripieno (It., rē-p'yâ′nŏh). "Filling up"; "supplementary." 1. A *ripieno* part supports the leading orchestral parts by doubling them or by filling in the harmony.—2. In scores, *ripieno* is a direction calling for the entrance of the full string section.

Riposo, con (It., kŏhn rē-pô´sŏh). In a calm, tranquil manner; reposefully.

Riprendere (It., rē-pren´dĕh-rĕh). To resume; *stringendo per riprendere il 1° tempo*, hastening, in order to regain the former tempo.

Risentito (It., rē-sen-tē´tŏh). Energetic, vigorous; expressive.

Risoluto (It., rē-sŏh-loo´tŏh). In a resolute, vigorous, decided style.

Risvegliato (It., rē-svāl-yah´tŏh). Lively, animated.

Ritardando (It., rē-tar-dăhn´dŏh). Growing slower and slower.

Ritardare, senza (It., sen´tsăh rē-tar-dah´rĕh). Without slackening the pace.

Ritenuto (It., rē-tĕh-noo´tŏh). Held back; at a slower rate of speed.

Ritmico (It., rit´mē-kŏh). Rhythmical; MISURATO.

Ritmo (It,. rit´mŏh). Rhythm.

Ritornello (It., rē-tor-nel´lŏh). 1. The burden of a song.—2. A repeat.—3. In accompanied vocal works, an instrumental prelude, interlude, or postlude (refrain).—In a concerto, the orchestral refrain.

Rock. A term that covers a variety of popular styles of the 1960s–70s; *acid rock, folk rock, hard rock, jazz rock, mellow rock, punk rock,,* etc. It is an outgrowth of the ROCK 'N' ROLL of the 1950s, but features amplified guitars and keyboards.

Rock 'n' roll. A popular American style of the 1950s that emerged from the black ethnic style of RHYTHM AND BLUES. Rock 'n' roll featured a percussively heavy reinforcement of the meter (beat) played by JAZZ-like combos consisting of tenor saxophone, piano, bass, drums, and sometimes guitar. BLUES harmonic structures were common, but without the characteristic BLUE NOTES or blues mood.

Rococo. A term descriptive of the ornamental type of composition current from about 1725 to 1775.

Roll. 1. A tremolo or trill on the drum. . . *Long roll,* the prolonged and reiterated drum signal to troops, for attack or rally.—2. In organ playing, a rapid arpeggio.—3. On the tambourine, a rapid and reiterated stroke with the knuckles.

Romance. Originally, a ballad, or popular tale in verse, in the Romance dialect; now a title for epico-lyrical songs, or of short sentimental or romantic instrumental pieces without special form.—The French romance is a simple love ditty.

Romanesca. A type of 17th-century Italian court dance.

Romantic. In music history, the period from about 1815 to c. 1910, overlapping with late Classicism on one end, and Impressionism and Expressionism on the other end.

Romanza. Italian term for a short romantic song or a solo instrumental piece.

Rondeau. A medieval French song with instrumental accompaniment, consisting of an aria and a choral refrain.

Rondo. An instrumental piece in which the leading theme is repeated, alternating with the others. A typical pattern, with letters representing thematic section, would be: A-B-A-C-A-B-A.

Root. The lowest note of a chord in the fundamental position.

Rota. A round; also a Latin name for a *hurdy-gurdy*.

Roulade (Fr., roo-lähd´). A grace consisting of a run or *arpeggio* from one principal melody tone to another; a vocal or instrumental flourish.

Roulante. French for rolling; *caisse roulante* is a tenor drum.

Round. A vocal canon at the unison, without coda.

Rubato (It., roo-bäh´tŏh). "Robbed"; meaning "dwell on, and prolong prominent melody tones or chords." This requires an equivalent acceleration of less prominent tones, which are thus "robbed" of a portion of their time value.

Ruhig (Ger., roo´ĭyh). Quiet, calm, tranquil.

Rührung (Ger., rü-rŏŏng^k). Emotion.

Rumba. A syncopated Cuban dance popular in the United States in the 1930s–50s.

Run. A rapid scale passage; in vocal music, usually such a passage sung to one syllable.

S

S. Stands for *Segno* in the phrases *al Segno, dal Segno;* for *Senza, Sinistra, Solo, Soprano, Sordini;* and for *Subito* in the phrase *Volti subito* (V.S.).

Sackbut. An early form of trombone.

Saite (Ger., zā′tĕ). A string.

Salmo. Italian for psalm.

Salsa. "Sauce," Latin American dance music genre.

Saltarella, Saltarello (It., săhl-tăh-rel′lăh, -lŏh). A second division in many 16th- century dance tunes, in triple time, the skipping step marked in the rhythm

—Also, an Italian dance in $\frac{3}{4}$ or $\frac{6}{8}$ time.

Salto (It., săhl′tŏh). Leap; *di salto,* by a leap or leaps.—Also, skip or "cut."

Samba. Popular dance from Brazil.

Sanctus. See MASS.

Sanft (Ger., zăhnft). Soft, low.

Sans (Fr., săhn). Without.

Sarabande. A stately dance of Spanish or Asian origin. The instrumental *S.* has usually two 8-measure reprises, in slow tempo and triple time; its place in the Suite, as the slowest movement, is before the Gigue.

Sardana. A rapid, rustic dance of Catalonia.

Sarrusophone. A brass wind instrument with a double reed, invented in 1863.

Satz (Ger., săhtz). Movement, as of a sonata or symphony.

Sautillé (Fr., soh-tē-yā′). Technique of string playing with a bouncing bow.

Saxhorn. A brass wind instrument invented c. 1840 by Sax. It is essentially an improved key bugle or ophicleide, having from 3 to 5 valves instead of keys.

Saxophone. A metal wind instrument invented c. 1840 by Adolphe Sax, having a clarinet mouthpiece with single reed, the key mechanism and fingering also resembling those of the clarinet. It has a mellow, penetrating tone.

Scale. 1. The series of tones that form, *(a)* any major or minor key (*diatonic* scale), or *(b)* the *chromatic* scale of successive semitonic steps.—2. In the tubes of wind instruments (especially organ pipes), the ratio between width of bore and length.

Scat singing. A type of jazz performance in which a singer improvises nonsense words, sometimes imitating the sounds produced by musical instruments.

Scena (It., shâ´năh). An accompanied dramatic solo, consisting of arioso and recitative passages, and often ending with an aria.

Schalkhaft (Ger., shăhlk´hăft). Roguish, sportive, wanton.

Schallplatte (Ger., shăhl´-plăht-tĕ). Phonograph record.

Schaurig (Ger., show´rĭyh). In a style expressive of mortal dread, weirdly.

Schelmisch (Ger., shĕl´mish). Joking, roguish.

Scherzando (It., skâr-tsăhn´dŏh). In a playful, sportive, toying manner; lightly.

Scherzo (It., skâr-tsŏh). A joke, jest.—1. An instrumental piece of a light, piquant, humorous character.—2. A vivacious movement, usually the third, in the symphony, with strongly marked rhythm and sharp, unexpected contrasts in rhythm and harmony.

Schietto (It., skē-et´tŏh). Simply, quietly; neatly, deftly.

Schlag (Ger., shlăyh). A beat or stroke; *Schlaginstrumente*, percussion instruments.

Schleppen (Ger., shlep´pen). To drag, retard.

Schluss (Ger., shlŏŏss). Close, cadence; end.

Schlüssel (Ger., shlüsel). Clef.

Schmachtend (Ger., shmah´tent). Languishing(ly), longing(ly).

Schmeichelnd (Ger., shmī´yhelnt). Flatteringly; in a coaxing, caressful style.

Schmelzend (Ger., shmel´tsĕnt). "Melting," lyrical.

Schmerzlich (Ger., shmârts´lĭyh). Painful(ly), sorrowful(ly), plaintive(ly).

Schmetternd (Ger., shmet´ternt). A term calling for brass instruments to be played with a blared or "brassy" tone.

Schnell (Ger., shnel). Fast, quick, rapid.

Schottische (shot´ish). A round dance in $\frac{2}{4}$ time, a variety of the Polka.

Schwach (Ger., shvăh). Weak; soft, faint, low.

Schwebend (Ger., shvā´bent). Floating, soaring; buoyant; in a lofty, elevated style.

Schwellen (Ger., shvel´len). To swell, as in an organ.

Schwer (Ger., shvār). Heavy, ponderous; difficult.

Schwermüt(h)ig (Ger., shvār´müˊtĭyh). Sad, melancholy.

Schwindend (Ger., shvin′dent). Dying away, *morendo.*

Schwungvoll (Ger., shvŏŏngᵏ′fŏhl). Swingingly; buoyantly; with sweep and passion.

Scintillante (It., shin-tĭl-lähn′těh). Sparkling, brilliant.

Sciolto, -a (It., shôl-tŏh, -täh). Freely, fluently, nimbly.

Scivolando (It., shē-vŏh-lähn′dŏh). Same as *Glissando*, in piano playing.

Scoop. Vocal tones are "scooped" when taken, instead of by a firm and just attack, by a rough *portamento* from a lower tone.

Scordatura (It., skŏhr-däh-too′räh). A change in the ordinary tuning of a string instrument, to obtain special effects or easier execution.

Score. A systematic arrangement of the vocal or instrumental parts of a composition on separate staves one above the other... *Closed* or *compressed score*, a Short score... *Full* or *orchestral score*, one in which each vocal and instrumental part has a separate staff... *Piano score*, a piano arrangement of an orchestral score, the words of any leading vocal parts being inserted *above* the music without their notes... *Short score*, any abridged arrangement or skeleton transcript; also, a 4-part vocal score on 2 staves... *Vocal score*, that of an *a cappella* composition; also, the vocal parts written out in full, usually on separate staves, the piano accompaniment being arranged or compressed (from the full instrumental score) on 2 staves below the rest.

Scoring. Instrumentation, orchestration.

Scorrevole (It., skŏhr-rā′vŏh-lěh). Fluent, flowing, gliding.

Scotch snap. The rhythmic motive ♪♩. found in many Scotch airs.

Sdegnoso (It., zdān-yoh′sŏh). In a style expressing scorn, disdain, or wrath.

Sdrucciolando (It., zdrŏŏt-chŏh-lähn′dŏh). Sliding, *glissando.*

Se (It., sā.) If... *Se bisogna*, if necessary... *Se piace*, if you please.

Sec (Fr., sek). Dry, simple.

Secco (It., sek′kŏh). Dry, simple; not dwelt on... *Recitativo secco*, one with a simple figured-bass accompaniment.

Sécheresse, avec (Fr., äh-věk sā-shŭ-ress′). Dryly; without dwelling on or embellishing.

Second. 1. The interval between 2 conjunct degrees.—2. The alto part or voice.—3. Performing a part lower in pitch than first, as second bass, second violins.—4. Lower in pitch, as second string.—5. Higher; as second line of staff.

Secondary chords. Subordinate chords.

Secondo, -a (It., sěh-kŏhn′dŏh, -däh). Second; also a second part or performer in a duet.

Section. A short division (one or more periods) of a composition, having distinct rhythmic and harmonic boundaries; specifically, half a phrase.

Secular music. Music other than that intended for worship or devotional purposes.

Seelenvoll (Ger., zeh´leh-fol). Soulfully.

Segno (t., sän´yŏh). A sign. . . *Al segno*, to the sign; *Dal segno*, from the sign;—directions to the performer to turn back and repeat from the place marked by the sign (𝄋) to the word *Fine*, or to a double bar with hold (⌒).

Segue (It., sä´gwĕh). 1. Follows; *segue l'aria*, the aria follows.—2. Simile.

Seguendo (It., sĕh-gwen´dŏh). Following.

Seguidilla (Sp. sä-gwē-dē´yäh). A Spanish dance in triple time, some varieties being slow, others lively; usually in minor, accompanied by guitar and voice, and at times by the castanets.

Sehnsüchtig (Ger., zän´züyh´tïyh). Longingly; in a style expressive of yearning.

Sehr (Ger., zär). Very.

Semibreve. A whole note.

Semiquaver. Sixteenth note.

Semitone. A half tone.

Semplice (It., sem´plē-chĕh). In a simple, natural, unaffected style.

Sempre (It., sem´prĕh). Always, continually; throughout.

Sensibile (It., sen-sē´bē-lĕh). Audible; sensitive. . . *Nota sensibile*, leading note.

Sentito (It., sen-tē´tŏh). With feeling, expression, special emphasis.

Senza (It., sen´tsäh). Without. (Abbreviated S.)—*Senza di slentare*, without retarding. . . *S. misura*, "without measure," that is, not in strict time. . . *S. passione*, without passion, quietly. . . *S. rallentare*, without retarding. . . *S. suono*, "without tone," that is, spoken.

Septet. A concerted composition for seven voices or instruments.

Septuor (Fr., sep-tü-ohr´). A septet.

Septuplet. A group of 7 equal notes to be performed in the time of 4 or 6 of the same kind in the regular rhythm.

Sequence. 1. The repetition, at different pitch levels, more often than twice in succession, of a melodic motive.—2. In the Catholic Church, a kind of hymn.

Serenade. 1. An "evening song"; especially such a song sung by a lover before his lady's window.—2. An instrumental composition imitating the above in style.

Serenata (It., sĕh-rĕh-nah´täh). 1. A species of dramatic cantata in vogue during the 18th century.—2. An instrumental composition midway between Suite and Symphony, but freer in form than either, having 5, 6, or more movements, and in chamber music style.—3. See SERENADE.

Sereno (It., sĕh-rā´nŏh). In a serene, tranquil style.

Serial music. A 20th-century technique of composition in which all thematic materials are derived from a series of 12 different notes of the chromatic scale, graduated dynamics, a set of different rhythms, and different instrumental timbres. Serial music represents an expansion of the 12-tone method of composition into the domain of note values, dynamics, and instrumental timbres.

Serietà, con (It., kŏhn sĕh-rē-ĕh-tah´). Seriously.

Serio, -a (It., sâ´rē-ŏh, -ăh). Serious. . . *Opera seria,* grand or tragic opera.

Serpent. A bass wind instrument invented by Canon Guillaume of Auxerre in 1590.

Serré (Fr., sĕh-rā´, *pressed*). Playing faster and with more excitement.

Settimino (It., set-tē-mē´nŏh). A septet.

Seventeenth. Interval of 2 octaves plus a third.

Seventh chord. A chord of the 7th, composed of a root with its 3rd, 5th, and 7th.

Severo (It., sĕh-vâ´rŏh). Strictlly; rigidly observing tempo and expression marks.

Sext. 1. The interval of a sixth.—2. The office of the fourth Canonical Hour.

Sextet. A concerted composition for 6 voices or instruments, or for 6 *obbligato* voices with instrumental accompaniment.

Sextuplet. A group of 6 equal notes to be performed in the time of 4 of the same kind in the regular rhythm.

Sfogato (It., sfŏh-gah´tŏh). "Exhaled"; a direction to sing lightly and airily.

Sforzato (It., sfŏhr-tsah´tŏh). A direction to perform the tone or chord with special stress, or marked and sudden emphasis.

Sfumato (It., sfŏŏ-mah´tŏh). Very lightly, like a vanishing smoke wreath.

Shading. In the interpretation of a composition, the combination and alternation of any or all the varying degrees of tone power between *fortissimo* and *pianissimo*, for obtaining artistic effect.

Shake. A trill.

Shanty. A work song of the English working class, particularly of sailors.

Sharp. 1. The character ♯, which raises the pitch of the note before which it is set by a semitone; the Double sharp, symbolized by a cross or the letter X, raises the note by 2 semitones.—2. Too high in pitch.—3. (Of intervals.) Major or augmented.—4. Having a sharp or sharps in the key signature.

Shawm. A medieval high-pitched wind instrument.

Shift. In playing the violin, etc., a change by the left hand from the first position; the 2nd position is called the *half-shift*, the 3rd the *whole shift*, and the 4th the *double shift*.

Si (It., sē). 1. The 7th solmization syllable.—2. One; it.

Siciliana (It., sē-chē-lē-ah'näh). Dance of the Sicilian peasants; a kind of pastorale in moderately slow tempo and $\frac{6}{8}$ or $\frac{12}{8}$ time, frequently in minor.

Side drum. See SNARE DRUM.

Sight reading. An ability to read unfamiliar music with ease. In singing, it is synonymous with solfeggio.

Signal horn. A bugle.

Signature. The signs set at the head of the staff at the beginning of a piece or movement; the *Key signature* is the chromatic sign or signs (sharps or flats); the *Time signature* is the figures or signs indicating the measure.

Similar motion. Motion of voices in the same direciton, as distinguished from contrary motion.

Simile (It., sē'mē-lĕh). Similarly; a direction to perform the following measures or passages in the same style as the preceding.

Simple. Not compound.

Sinfonia (It., sin-fôh-nē'äh). 1. A symphony.—2. An opera overture.

Sinfonie (Ger., sin-fôh-nē'). Symphony.

Sinfonietta (It., sin-fôh-nē-ĕt'ah). A small symphony, sometimes for a chamber orchestra.

Singend (Ger., zing'ent). Singing, melodious, *cantabile*.

Singspiel (Ger., zing^k'shpēl). A type of German opera established during the 18th century; usually light, and characterized by spoken interludes.

Singstimme (Ger., zing^k'shtim'mē). The singing voice; the voice.

Sinistra (It., sē-nĭ'sträh). Left.

Sino (It., sē'nôh). To, up to, as far as, till. . . *Sino* (or *sin*) *al fine*, to the end.

Sitar. A string instrument of India, in the shape of a lute, plucked with a plectrum.

Sixth. Interval containing 6 diatonic degrees.

Sixteenth note. Half the value of an eighth note.

Sixth chord. First inversion of a triad.

Six-four chord. Second inversion of a triad.

Skip. Melodic progression by an interval wider than a Second; *disjunct* progression.

Slancio, con (It., kŏhn zlăhn´chŏh). With dash, vehemence; impetuously.

Slargando (It., zlar-găhn´dŏh). Slower; *più sostenuto.*

Slentando (It., zlen-tăn´dŏh). Growing slower.

Slide. 1. The movable U-shaped tube in the trombone, etc.—2. Three or four swiftly ascending or descending scale tones.—3. On a violin bow, that part of the nut that slides along the stick.

Slur. A curved line under or over 2 or more notes, signifying that they are to be played *legato.* In vocal music the slur unites notes to be sung in one breath; the notes so sung are called a *slur.*

Sminuendo (It., zmē-nŏŏ-en´dŏh). Same as DIMINUENDO.

Smorzando (It., zmŏhr-tsăhn´dŏh). Dying away.

Snare drum. A side drum, across the lower head of which are stretched several gut strings, the "snares," whose jarring against the head reinforces the tone.

Soave (It., sŏh-ah´vĕh). Suavely, sweetly, softly, flowingly.

Soft pedal. The left pedal on the piano reducing the sound by shifting the keyboard, so that only 2 of the 3 strings in the middle register of the piano are struck by the hammers.

Soggetto (It., sŏhd-jet´tŏh). Subject, theme.

S

Sognando (It., sŏhn-yăhn´dŏh). Dreaming, dreamily.

Soh. Stands for *Sol,* in Tonic Sol-fa.

Sol (It., sôl). The fifth of the Aretinian syllables, and name of the note *G* in France, Italy, etc.

Solenne (It., sŏh-len´nĕh). Solemn, in a lofty style.

Sol-fa. 1. To sing *solfeggi,* especially to the solmization syllables.—2. Solmization, and the syllables sung in it.

Solfeggio (It., sŏhl-fed´jŏh; plural *solfeggi* [-jē]). A vocal exercise either on one vowel, or on the solmization syllables, or to words.

Soli (It., soh´lē). The plural of solo in Italian.

Solito (It., sô´lē-tŏh). Accustomed, habitual. . . *Al solito,* as usual.

Solmization. A method of teaching the scales and intervals by syllables, the invention of which is ascribed to Guido d'Arezzo (11th century). It was based on the hexachord, or 6-tone scale; the first 6 tones of the major scale, *c d e f g a*, were named *ut, re, mi, fa, sol, la.* The 7th syllable *si*, for the leading tone, was added during the 17th century; about the same time, the name *ut* for *C* was changed to *do*, except in France.

Solo (It., soh´lŏh). Alone.—*Solo* is a piece or passage for a single voice or instrument, or in which one voice or instrument predominates. In orchestral scores, "Solo" marks a passage where one instrument takes a leading part.

Sombre (Fr., sŏhn´br). Dark, veiled, obscure.

Sommo, -a (It., sŏhm´mŏh, -mäh). Utmost, highest, greatest, extreme.

Son (Fr., sŏhn). Sound; tone.

Sonata (It., sŏh-nah´täh). An instrumental composition in 3 or 4 extended movements contrasted in theme, tempo, and mood; usually for a solo instrument or chamber ensemble.

Sonata form. (Also known as *sonata allegro form* and *first movement form.*) The procedure usually used for first movements of Classical symphonies, sonatas, and chamber works; it may be used for other movements as well.

Sonatina (It., sŏh-näh-tē´näh). A short sonata in 2 or 3 (rarely 4) movements, the first in the characteristic first-movement form, abbreviated.

Song. A short poem with a musical setting characterized by a structure in simple periods. There are *Folk songs* and *Art songs*; the latter may be either *strophic* (each strophe sung to the same tune, with a change at most in the final one), or *through-composed.*

Song form. A form of composition, either vocal or instrumental, that has 3 sections and 2 themes, the second (contrasting) theme occupying the 2nd section.

S

Sonoro, -a (It., sŏh-nô´rŏh, -räh). Sonorously, resoundingly, resonantly, ringingly.

Sopra (It., soh´prah). Upon; above, over; higher. . . In piano music, *sopra* written in the part for either hand means that that hand is to reach *over* the other.

Sopranino (It., soh-prah-nē´nŏh). "Little soprano"; the highest pitch of the soprano register, as in sopranino saxophones, and sopranino recorders.

Soprano (It., sŏh-prah´nŏh). The highest class of the human voice; the female soprano, or *treble*, has a normal compass from c^1 to a^2; solo voices often reach above c^3, some as high as c^4. . . *Soprano clef*, the C clef on the first line.

Sordamente (It., sŏhr-däh-men´tĕh). With a veiled, muffled tone.

Sordino (It., sŏhr-dē´nŏh). 1. A mute; *con sordini*, with mutes; *senza sordini*, without mutes; *si levano i sordini*, take off the mutes.—2. Damper (of the piano).

Sospirando (It., sŏh-spē-**rä**hn´dŏh). Sighing, sobbing; catching the breath.

Sostenuto (It., sŏh-stĕh-noo´tŏh). Sustained, prolonged.—Standing alone, as a tempo mark, it is much the same as *Andante cantabile*; it may also imply a *tenuto*, or a uniform rate of decreased speed.— *Sostenuto pedal*, sustaining pedal.

Sotto (It., sŏht´tŏh). Below, under. . . In piano music, *sotto* written in the part for either hand means that that hand is to play (reach) *under* the other. . . (*Sotto voce*), in an undertone, aside, under the breath.

Soubrette (Fr., soo-bret´). In comedy and comic opera, a maidservant of intriguing and coquettish character; also applied to various similar light roles.

Soul. A style of black rhythm-and-blues singing.

Soundboard. The thin plate of wood placed below or behind the strings of various instruments to reinforce and prolong their tones.

Sound hole. A hole cut in the belly of a string instrument.

Soundpost. In the violin, etc., the small cylindrical wooden prop set inside the body, between belly and back, just behind the treble foot of the bridge.

Sousaphone. A spiral type of bass tuba, which is coiled around the player, with a large bellow turned forwards.

Space. In the staff, the interval between two lines or ledger lines.

Spasshaft (Ger., shpahs´hähft). *Scherzando.*

Spianato, -a (It., sp'yä-nah´tŏh, -täh). Smooth, even, tranquil.

Spiccato (It., spik-kah´tŏh). Sharp staccato. See SPRINGING BOW.

Spigliatezza (It., spē-l-yäh-tet´säh). Agility, dexterity.

Spinet (spin´et). An obsolete keyboard string instrument, like a harpsichord but smaller.

Spinto (It., spin´toh). Compelled, intense; applied to a high voice in expressive emotional opera parts.

Spiritoso (It., spē-rē-toh´sŏh). Spiritedly; with spirit, animation, energy.

Spiritual. A religious song cultivated by black slaves in the pre-Civil War South.

Spitze (Ger., shpit-sĕ). 1. Point (of the bow).—2. Toe (in organ playing).

Spitzig (Ger., shpit´zǐyh). Sharp, pointed.

Sprechstimme (Ger., shpreh´shtim-mĕ). Literally, "speech song"; inflected spoken singing, with pitches indicated approximately on the music staff.

Springing bow. In violin playing, a style of bowing in which the bow is allowed to drop on the string, making it rebound and quit the string between each two notes. There are two varieties: (1) The *Spiccato*, indicated by dots over the notes, and played near the middle of the bow with a loose wrist, for rapid passages in equal notes, employing the wrist stroke throughout for each detached note; (2) the *Saltato*, with a longer fall and higher rebound, generally employed when several equal *staccato* notes are to be taken in one bow.

Square dance. A parlor or country dance, such as a quadrille, performed by several couples in a square formation.

Stabat Mater (L., stăh′băht măh′tĕr). A Latin sequence on the Crucifixion sung in the Roman Catholic liturgy.

Stabile (It., stah′bē-lĕh). Steady, firm.

Staccato (It., stăhk-kah′tŏh). Detached, separated; a style in which the notes played or sung are more or less abruptly disconnected.

Staccato mark. A dot or wedge-shaped stroke over a note, the former indicating a less abrupt *staccato* than the latter; the *Mezzo-staccato* is indicated by dotted notes under a slur.

Staff. The 5 parallel lines used in modern notation; Plainchant uses only 4. . . *Staff notation*, the staff and all musical signs connected with it.

Stanco, -a (It., stăhn′kŏh, -kăh). Weary, dragging.

Ständchen (Ger, shtän′yhĕn). Serenade.

Stanza. A symmetric unit of a song.

Stark (Ger., shtark). Loud, forcible; *forte*.

Steg (Ger., shteg). The bridge on string instruments; *am Steg*, bowing near the bridge.

Stem. The vertical line attached to a note head.

Stentato (It., sten-tah′tŏh). Retarded, dragged.

Step. A melodic progression of a second.—Also, a degree. . . *Chromatic step*, progression of a chromatic Second. . . *Diatonic step*, progression between neighboring tones of any diatonic scale. . . *Half step*, step of a semitone. . . *Whole step*, step of a whole tone.

Sterbend (Ger., shtär′bent). Dying; *morendo*.

Stesso (It., stes′sŏh). The same. . . *Lo stesso movimento*, the same movement.

Stile (It., stē′lĕh). Style. . . *Stile osservato*, strict style, especially of pure vocal music. . . *Stile rappresentativo*, dramatic monophonic song with instrumental accompaniment in chords; a late-16th-century kind of operatic recitative.

Stimme (Ger., shtim′mĕ). 1. Voice.—2. Part; *mit der Stimme*, COLLA PARTE.

Stimmung (Ger., shtim´mŏŏng[k]). 1. Tuning, pitch. . . *Stimmung halten*, to keep in tune.—2. Mood, frame of mind. . . *Stimmungsbild*, a "mood picture."

Stinguendo (It., stin-gwen´dŏh). Dying away.

Stiracchiato (It., stē-rӑhk-k'yah´tŏh). Dragging, delaying.

Stop. 1. That part of the organ mechanism that admits and "stops" the flow of wind to the grooves beneath the pipes.—2. A set or row of organ pipes of like character, arranged in graduated succession. These are called *speaking* or *sounding* stops. they are classed as *Flue work* (having flue pipes), and *Reed work* (having reed pipes).—3. *(a)* On the violin, etc., the pressure of a finger on a string, to vary the latter's pitch; a *double stop* is when 2 or more strings are so pressed and sounded simultaneously; *(b)* on wind instruments with fingerholes, the closing of a hole by finger or key to alter the pitch; *(c)* on wind instruments of the trumpet family, the partial closing of the bell by inserting the hand.

Stopped notes. Tones obtained by stopping; opposed to *open*.

Stopped pipes. Organ pipes closed at the top; opposed to *open*.

Strappare (It., strӑhp-pah´rӗh). To pluck off; in piano playing, to throw off a note or chord by a rapid, light turn of the wrist.

Strascinando (It., strӑh-shē-nӑhn´dŏh). Dragging, drawling. . . *Strascinando l'arco*, drawing the bow so as to bind the tones.

Stravagante (It., strӑh-vӑh-gӑhn´tӗh). Extravagant, fantastic, whimsical.

Streichinstrumente (Ger., shtriyh´in-stroo-men´tӗ). Bowed instruments.

Streng (Ger., Shtreng[k]). Severe(ly), strict(ly).

Strepitoso (It., strӗh-pē-toh´sŏh). In a noisy, boisterous, impetuous style.

Stretch. On a keyboard instrument, a wide interval or spread chord whose tones are to be taken simultaneously by the fingers of one hand.

Strettissimo (It., stret-tis´sē-mŏh). Very hurriedly.

Stretto (It. stret´tŏh). 1. A division of a fugue (usually a final development, for the sake of effect) in which subject and answer follow in such close succession as to overlap.—2. Pressed together, narrowed; hurried. . . *Andante stretto*, same as *Andante agitato*. . . *Stretto pedale*, the quick, deft shifting of the loud piano pedal, in a strongly marked chord passage, so that the harmonies may be at once forcible and distinct.

Strict style. A style of composition in which (most) dissonances are regularly prepared and resolved.

String. A tone-producing cord. . . *First string*, the highest of a set. . . *Open string*, one not stopped or shortened. . . *The Strings*, the string group in the orchestra.

String instruments. All instruments whose tones are produced by strings, whether struck, plucked, or bowed.

Stringendo (It., strin-jen´dŏh). Hastening, accelerating the movement, usually suddenly and rapidly, with a *crescendo.*

String quartet. A quartet for 1st and 2nd violin, viola, and 'cello.

String quintet. A quintet for 2 violins, 2 violas, and 'cello; or for 2 violins, 1 viola, and 2 'cellos; or for 2 violins, viola, 'cello, and double bass.

Strisciando (It., strē-shăhn´dŏh). Gliding, smooth, *legato, glissando.*

Strophic composition. See Song.

Strumento (It., stru-men´toh). Italian word for instruments.

Stück (Ger., shtük). A piece; a number.

Study. An etude, a teaching piece.

Sturm und Drang (Ger., stoorm ŏŏnt drahng). "Storm and stress"; a literary term borrowed to describe an emotional, minor-key style that emerged in the 1770s.

Style galant (Fr., stēl ga-lähn´). "Elegant" style of composition, emphasizing entertainment value, popular in the second half of the 18th century.

Su (It., soo). On, upon, by, near. . . *Arco in su*, up-bow.

Subdominant. The tone below the dominant in a diatonic scale; the 4th degree.

Subito (It, soo´bē-tŏh). Suddenly, without pause. . . *Volti subito*, turn over (the page) quickly. . . *p subito* (after *f*), an abrupt change to *piano*, without gradation.

Subject. A melodic motive or phrase on which a composition or movement is founded; a theme.

Submediant. The 3rd scale tone below the tonic; the 6th degree.

Suboctave. 1. The octave below a given tone.—2. The double contra-octave.

Subordinate chords. Chords not fundamental or principal; the triads on the 2nd, 3rd, 6th, and 7th degrees, and all seventh chords but the dominant 7th.

Substitution. In contrapuntal progression, the resolution or preparation of a dissonance by substituting, for the regular tone of resolution or preparation, its higher or lower octave in some other part.

Subtonic. The leading note.

Sugli (It., sool´yē), **Sui** (It., soo´ē). On the; near the.

Suite (Fr., süē´t´). 1. See Classical suite.—2. See Divertimento.

Suivez (Fr., süē-vā´). 1. Same as Colla parte.—2. "Continue," "go on."

Sul, sull', sulla, sulle (It.). On the, near the. . . *Sulla corda La*, on the *A* string. . . *Sulla tastiera*, near or by the fingerboard. . . *Sul ponticello*, near the bridge.

Suonare (It., sŏŏ-ô-näh´rĕh). Old form of the verb *sonare*, "to sound," "to play."

Superdominant. The 6th degree of a diatonic scale.

Supertonic. The 2nd degree of a diatonic scale.

Supplicando (IIt., sŏŏp-plē-kähn´dŏh). In a style expressive of supplication, entreaty, pleading.

Suspension. A dissonance caused by suspending (holding back) a tone or some tones of a chord while the other tones progress.

Süss (Ger., züss). Sweet(ly).

Sustain. To hold during the full time value; also, to perform in *sostenuto* style.

Sustaining pedal. A piano pedal that holds up dampers already raised by depressed keys, thus prolonging the tones of strings affected.

Susurrando (It., sŏŏ-sŏŏr-rähn´dŏh). In a whispering, murmuring tone.

Svanirando (It., zväh-nē-rähn´dŏh). Vanishing; fainter and fainter.

Svelto (It, zvel´tŏh). Light, nimble.

Swell. 1. In the organ, a set of pipes enclosed in a box with movable shutters that are opened and closed by a pedal.—2. A *crescendo*, or *crescendo* and *diminuendo*.

Swing. A smooth, sophisticated style of jazz playing, popular in the 1930s. Its distinctive characteristic was a trend towards a well-organized ensemble of professional instrumentalists. The main musical outline was established during rehearsals, but jam sessions were freely interpolated, with extended solos.

Syllabic melody. One each tone of which is sung to a separate syllable.

Syllable name. A syllable taken as the name of a note or tone; as *Do* for *C*.

Sympathetic strings. Strings stretched below or above the principal strings of lutes and other instruments to provide sympathetic resonance and thus enhance the sounds.

Symphonic. Resembling, or relating or pertaining to, a symphony. . . *Symphonic poem*, an extended orchestral composition that follows in its development the thread of a story or the ideas of a poem, repeating and interweaving its themes appropriately; it has no fixed form, nor set divisions like those of the symphony.

Symphonie (Fr., sahn-fŏh'nē). SYMPHONY.

Symphony. An orchestral composition in from 3 to 5 distinct "movements," or divisions, each with its own theme or themes and its own development.

Syncopation. The shifting of accents from strong beat to weak beat, or to between beats.

Syrinx. Panpipes.

S

T

T. Stands for *Tasto, Tempo, Tenor, Tre,* (T.C. = *tre corde*), and *Tutti*.

Tablature. 1. The rules and regulations for the poetry and song of the *Meistersinger.*—2. Early musical notation for the lute, viol, and organ.

Tabor. A small drum accompanying a folk singer, and tapped with only one hand.

Tacet. Latin for "it is silent"; a common usage in orchestral parts to mark a movement in which an instrument in question is not playing.

Tafelmusik (Ger., tăh'fel-moo-zik). "Table music"; music performed informally at a dinner gathering.

Tail. Same as STEM.

Takt (Ger., tăhkt). A beat; a measure; time... *Streng im Takt,* strictly in time.

Talea (L., tăh'lā-ŭ). See ISORHYTHM.

Talon (Fr. tah-lohn'). The end of the bow of the violin; literally, "heel."

Tambour (Fr., tahn-bŏŏr). Drum.

Tambour de basque (Fr., —duh băhsk). A tambourine.

Tambourine. A small, shallow drum with one parchment head, played by striking with the hand. Around the hoop are several pairs of loose metallic plates called *jingles*.

Tambour militaire (Fr., —mē-lē-tarh'). A military drum; a side drum.

Tam-tam. A large gong with deep resonance.

Tango. An Argentinian dance, characterized by strongly marked syncopation; became popular in ballrooms in the U.S. and Europe around 1912.

Tanto (It., tăhn'tŏh). As much, so much; too (much).

Tanz (Ger., tăhnts). A dance.

Tarantella (It., tăh-răhn-tel'lăh). A South Italian dance in § time, with gradually increasing tempo, and alternating between major and minor modes.—Also, a very rapid instrumental piece in ⅜ or § time, in bold and brilliant style.

Tardo (It., tăr'dŏh). Slow, lingering.

Tastiera (It., tăh-stē-â'răh). Keyboard; fingerboard... *Sulla tastiera,* on (near) the fingerboard.

Tasto (It., tăh'stŏh). Key; fret; touch; fingerboard; *sul tasto,* on (near) the fingerboard... *Tasto solo* means that the bass part is to be played, either as written or in octaves, without chords.

Te. Stands for *Si*, in Tonic Sol-fa.

Tedesco, -a (It., těh-děh´sköh, -skäh). German. . . *Alla tedesca*, in the German style (in waltz rhythms, with changing tempo).

Teil (Ger., tile). A part or section; a movement.

Tema (It., tā´mäh). Theme.

Temperament. A system of tuning in which tones of very nearly the same pitch, like *C* sharp and *D* flat, are made to sound alike by slightly "tempering" them (that is, slightly raising or lowering them).

Temple block. A hollow block of resonant wood that is struck by a drumstick; a set usually consists of five blocks tuned in a pentatonic scale.

Tempo (It., tem´pŏh). 1. Rate of speed, movement.—2. Time, measure. . . A TEMPO, return to the preceding pace. . . *Sempre in tempo*, always at the same pace; *in tempo misurato*, in strict time (after "*a piacere*"). . . *Tempo commodo*, at a convenient pace. . . *Tempo giusto*, at a proper, appropriate pace. . . *Tempo rubato*, see RUBATO. . . *L'istesso tempo*, or *Lo stesso tempo*, the same tempo; indicates, at a change of rhythm, that the pace remains the same. . . *Senza tempo*, same as A PIACERE. . . *Tempo primo*, at the original pace.

Tempo mark. A word or phrase indicating the rate of speed at which a piece should be performed.

Tenero (It., tâ´něh-rŏh). Tenderly, with tender emotion; delicately, softly.

Tenor. The high natural male voice; the *dramatic tenor*, of full and powerful quality, has a range from *c* to *b¹b; the lyric tenor*, sweeter and less powerful, from *d* to *c²*.—2. The viola.—3. A prefix to the names of instruments of similar compass; as *tenor trombone*.

Tenor clef. The *C* clef on the 4th line.

Tenore (It., těh-noh´rěh). Tenor.

Tenth. The diatonic interval of an octave plus 2 degrees.

Tenuto (It., těh-noo´tŏh). "Held"; means *(a)* generally, to sustain a tone for its full time value; *(b)* occasionally, *legato*. . . *Tenuto mark*, a short stroke over a note.

Ternary. Composed of, or progressing by, threes. . . *Ternary form*, Rondo form. . . *Ternary measure*, simple triple time.

Terz (Ger., târts). The interval of a third.

Tessitura (It., tes-sē-too´räh). The range covered by the main body of the tones of a given part, not including infrequent high or low tones. In English we say that the part "lies" high or low.

Tetrachord. The interval of a perfect fourth; the four scale tones contained in a perfect fourth.

Text. Words to which music is set.

Thematic composition. A style based on the contrapuntal treatment or development of one or more themes. (Invention, Fugue, Canon.)

Theme. A Subject.—Specifically, an extended and rounded-off subject with accompaniment, in period form, proposed as a foundation for elaborate variations.

Theme and variations. A form of composition in which the principal theme is clearly and explicitly stated at the beginning, and is then followed by a number of variations.

Theorbo. A kind of large, double-necked bass lute.

Thesis. Downbeat, strong beat. See ARSIS.

Third. An interval embracing 3 degrees. Also, the third degree of the scale, the Mediant.

Third stream jazz. The effort by some JAZZ musicians and art composers in the 1950s–60s to fuse elements of jazz and contemporary art music.

Thirteenth. An interval embracing an octave and a sixth; a compound sixth.

Thirty-second note. Half of the value of a sixteenth note.

Thorough bass. See BASSO CONTINUO.

Thumb position. The high positions in cello playing, where the thumb quits the neck of the instrument.

Tie. A curved line joining 2 notes of like pitch which are to be sounded as one note equal to their united time value.

Tierce (tērs). 1. Third.—2. One of the Canonical Hours.

Tierce de Picardie (Fr., t'yĕrs duh pē-kar′dē). PICARDY THIRD.

Timbale (Fr., tăn-băhl′). TIMPANI.

Timbre (Fr., tăn′br). Quality of tone.

Time. 1. The division of the measure into equal fractional parts of a whole note (*o*), thus regulating the accents and rhythmic flow of music. The sign for time is the *Time signature.* There are 2 classes of time, *Duple* and *Triple.* In *Duple time* the *number of beats* to the measure is divisible by 2; in *Triple time*, by 3. There are also 2 subclasses, *Compound Duple time* and *Compound Triple time*; in the former *each beat* contains a dotted note (or its equivalent in other notes or rests) divisible by 3; in the latter, not only the number of beats in each measure is divisible by 3, but also each beat, as above.

Timoroso (It., tē-mŏh-roh′sŏh). In a style expressive of timidity, hesitation, or fear.

Timpani (It., tim´päh-nē). An orchestral drum consisting of a hollow brass or copper hemisphere resting on a tripod, with a vellum head stretched by means of an iron ring and tightened by a set of screws, or by cords and braces. It is generally played in pairs, the large drum yielding any tone from *F* to *c*, and the smaller from *B*♭ to *f.*

Toccata (It., tŏhk-kah´täh). A composition for keyboard, free and bold in style, consisting of runs and passages alternating with fugued or contrapuntal work, generally in equal notes, with a flowing, animated, and rapid movement.

Tom-tom. Native American drum producing a dull but incisive tone.

Ton (Ger., tohn). A tone; key; mode; pitch; octave scale.

Tonada (Sp., tŏh-nah´däh). A generic name for a Spanish song or dance, also adopted in Latin America.

Tonadilla (Sp. tŏh-nah-dē´ya). A Spanish theater piece of a light genre.

Tonal. Pertaining to tones, or to a tone, mode, or key. . . *Tonal imitation,* imitation within the key of a composition; nonmodulating imitation.

Tonal answer. An answer to the subject in a fugue, in which the tonic is answered by the dominant and the dominant is answered by the tonic, thus altering the intervallic content of the theme.

Tonality. See KEY.

Tonart (Ger., tohn´art). Key (tonality).

Tondichtung (Ger., tohn´di**yh**-tŏŏng^k). Tone poem.

Tone. See ACOUSTICS. . . Half tone, a minor, or chromatic, second. . Whole tone, a major second.

Tone cluster. Several consecutive notes of the diatonic, pentatonic, or chromatic scale played simultaneously in a "cluster."

Tone color. Quality of tone.

Tone poem. See SYMPHONIC POEM.

Tone row. The fundamental subject in a 12-tone composition.

Tongue (*noun*). A reed; (*verb*) to employ the tongue in producing, modifying, or interrupting the tones of certain wind instruments.

Tonguing. The production of tone effects on wind instruments by the aid of the tongue. . . *Single tonguing,* the effect obtained by the repeated tongue thrust to the nearly inaudible consonant *t* or *d; Double tonguing,* that obtained by the repetition of *t k; Triple tonguing,* by *t k t,* etc.—FLUTTER-TONGUE.

Tonic. 1. The keynote of a scale.—2. The triad on the keynote (tonic chord).

Tonic Sol-fa. A method of teaching vocal music, invented by Sarah Ann Glover of Norwich, England, about 1812. Pupils are taught to recognize the tones of the scale by observing the mental impressions peculiar to each tone. It is based on the Movable Do system, and uses the syllables *doh, ray, me, fah, soh, lah, te.*

Tonkunst (Ger., tohn´künst). The art of music; *Tonkünstler,* composer.

Tonleiter (Ger., tohn´lī-ter). Scale.

Tonsatz (Ger., tohn´sähtz). A composition.

Tonus peregrinus. Latin for "wandering mode"; an excerpt of plainchant used in a choral work.

Tornando (It., tohr-nähn´dŏh). Returning; *tornando al primo tempo,* returning to the original tempo.

Tosto (It., tô´stŏh). Swift, bold; soon.

Touch. 1. The method and manner of applying the fingers to the keys of keyboard instruments.—2. The amount and kind of resistance overcome by the fingers in depressing the keys of an organ or piano; as a *heavy, light,* or *elastic touch.*

Touche (Fr., toosh). Fingerboard; *sur la touche,* to bow on the fingerboard.

Tranquillo (It., trähn-kwil´lŏh). Tranquilly, quietly, calmly.

Transcription. The arrangement or adaptation of a piece for some voice or instrument other than that for which it was originally intended.

Transient. Passing; not principal; intermediate. . . *Transient chord,* an intermediate chord foreign both to the key left and that reached.

Transition. 1. Modulation, especially a transient one.—2. In Tonic Sol-fa, a modulation without change of mode.

Transpose. To perform or write out a composition in a different key.

Transposing instruments. 1 Instruments whose natural scale is always written in *C* major, regardless of the actual pitch.—2. Instruments having some device by which the action or strings can be shifted so that higher or lower tones are produced than when they are in the normal pisiton.

Transverse flute. See FLUTE.

Trascinando (It. träh-shē-nähn´dŏh). Held back, retarded.

Trattenuto (It., träht-tĕh-noo´tŏh). Held back, retarded.

Trauermusik (Ger., trow´er-moo-zĭk). Funeral music.

Träumerisch (Ger,. troy´mĕrish). Dreamy.

Traurig (Ger., trow´rĭyh). Sad, melancholy.

Tre (It., trä). Three. . . *A tre,* for 3 voices or instruments; *a tre voci,* for 3 parts.

Treble. Soprano. . . *Treble clef,* the *G* clef: 🎼

Treibend (Ger., trī´bent). Urging, hastening.

Tremolando (It., trĕ-mŏh-lăhn´dŏh). With a tremolo effect.

Tremolo (It., trâ´mŏh-lŏh). A quivering, fluttering. 1. In singing, a tremulous, unsteady tone.—2. On bowed instruments, an effect produced by the very rapid alternation of down-bow and up-bow, written: —3. On the piano, the rapid alternation of the_tones of a chord.

Trepak (trĕh-pahk´). Russian dance in fast duple time.

Très (Fr., trā). Very; *molto.*

Triad. A "3-tone" chord composed of a given tone (the Root) with its third and fifth in ascending order in the scale.

Triangle. A steel rod bent into triangular shape, with one corner left slightly open; it is struck with a metal wand.

Trill. The even and rapid alternation of 2 tones a major or minor second apart; the lower tone is the *principal note,* the higher tone the *auxiliary.*

Trio (It., trē´ŏh). 1. A piece for 3 parts.—2. In minuets, marches, etc., the *trio* or *alternativo* is a second dance or march, after which the first is repeated.

Trio sonata. A type of Baroque chamber music written in 3 parts, the 2 upper parts supported by a figured bass.

Triolet (Fr., trē-ŏh-lā). Triplet.

Trionfale (It., trē-ŏhn-fah´ĕh). Triumphal.

Triple concerto. Concerto for 3 solo instruments and orchestra.

Triple counterpoint. See COUNTERPOINT.

Triplet. A group of 3 equal notes to be performed in the time of 2 of like value in the regular rhythm; written:

♩♩♩ or ♩♩♩ or ♩♩♩ or ♩♩♩

Tristo, -a (It., trī´stŏh, -stäh). In a style expressive of sadness or melancholy.

Tritone. The interval of 3 whole tones, or the augmented fourth:

🎼

Tromba (It., trŏm-băh´). Trumpet.

Tromba marina (It., —mah-rē´năh). A monochord, with a single string stretched over a very long wooden box, which was used in the Middle Ages for acoustical experiments, and which could easily produce a long series of harmonics.

Trombone. The middle instrument of the brass group, pitched below the trumpet and the horn and above the tuba.

Trommel (Ger., trôm´mel). Drum.

Trompette (Fr., trŏhm-pĕt´). Trumpet.

Tronco, -a (It., trŏhn´kŏh, -kăh). Cut off short; stopped abruptlly.

Trope. In medieval Roman liturgy, an insertion of a musical section, usually a hymn.

Troppo (It., trŏp´pŏh). Too, too much. . . *Allegro ma non troppo*, rapid, but not too fast.

Troubadours. A class of poet-musicians originating in Provence, and flourishing in France, Spain, and Italy from the 11th–13th centuries.

Trüb(e) (Ger., trüp, trü´bĕ). Gloomy, dismal; sad, melancholy.

Trumpet. A metal wind instrument with cupped mouthpiece and small bell; the tone is brilliant, penetrating, and of great carrying power. It is a transposing instrument; the ordinary compass is about 2 octaves.

Tuba. 1. The straight trumpet of the Romans.—2. A name applied to the 3 lowest members of the saxhorn family; they are metal wind instruments of ponderous tone, with a compass of some 4 octaves.

Tubular chimes. Metal bells made of long, hollow cylindrical tubes, suspended from a bar.

Tumultuoso (It., too-mŏŏl-too-oh´sŏh). Vehement, impetuous; agitated.

Tune. An air, melody; chiefly applied to short, simple pieces or familiar melodies.

Tuning. 1. The process of bringing an instrument into tune.—2. The *accordatura* of a string instrument. . . *Tuning fork*, a two-pronged instrument of metal, yielding one fixed tone (usually a^1 or c^2). . . *Tuning slide*, a sliding U-shaped section of the tube in certain brass instruments, used to adjust their pitch to that of other instruments.

Turn. A melodic grace consisting (usually) or 4 notes, a principal note (twice struck) with its higher and lower auxiliary. Sign ∾.

Tutti (It., too´tē). The indication in an orchestral or choral score that the entire orchestra, or chorus, is to enter; usually placed after an extended solo passage.

Twelfth. 1. The interval of an octave plus a fifth; a compound fifth.

Twelve-tone technique. See DODECAPHONY.

U

Über (Ger. , *ü*′ber). Over, above.

Übermässig (Ger., *ü*′ber-mä′s**ĭyh**). Augmented.

Übung (Ger., *ü*′bŏŏng**ᵏ**). Exercise; practice.

Ukulele. Popular guitar-type instrument.

Un (Fr., ön; It., oon), **Une** (Fr., ün), **Uno, -a** (It., oo′nŏh, -năh). One; a or an. . . *Un peu plus lent*, a little slower. . . *Una corda*, with the soft pedal.

Und (Ger., oont). And.

Ungebunden (Ger., ŏŏn′gĕ-bŏŏn′den). Unconstrained.

Ungeduldig (Ger., ŏŏn′gĕ-dŏŏl′d**ĭyh**). Impatient(ly).

Ungestüm (Ger., ŏŏn′gĕ-sht*üm*′). Impetuous(ly).

Unison. A tone of the same pitch as a given tone; also, a higher or lower octave of the given tone.

Unisono (It., oo-nē′sŏh-nŏh). Unison. . . *All' unisono*, progressing in unison with or in octave with.

Uniti (It., oo-nē′tē). This signifies, after "*divisi*," that the instruments or voices again perform their parts in unison.

Un poco (It., oon pô′kŏh). "A little," as in *un poco più lento*, a little more slowly.

Unruhig (Ger., ŏŏn′roo˜ĭyh). Restless(ly), unquiet(ly).

Unter (Ger., ŏŏn′ter). Under, below, sub-.

Upbeat. 1. The raising of the hand in beating time.—2. An unaccented part of a measure (see AUFTAKT).

Up-bow. The stroke of the bow in the direction from point to nut; the *Up-bow mark* is ∨ or ∧ .

Upright piano. A piano standing up, with its strings arranged diagonally along the vertical soundboard, as distinguished from a GRAND PIANO.

Ut. 1. The first of the solmization syllables.—2. Name of the note *C* in France.

V

V. Stands for *Vide, Violino, Volti,* and *Voce, Vv.,* for *Violini.*

Va (It., vah). Go on, continue. . . *Va crescendo,* go on increasing (in loudness).

Vaghezza, con (It., kŏhn văh-gĕt´tsăh). With charm.

Vago (It., văh´gŏh). Vague, dreamy.

Valse (Fr., văhls). Waltz.

Valve. In brass instruments, a device for diverting the air current from the main tube into an additional side tube, thus lengthening the air column and lowering the pitch of the instrument's scale. There are *Piston* valves and *Rotary* valves.

Valzer (It., văhl´tser). Waltz.

Vamp. Expression in popular music meaning to improvise an accompaniment.

Variation. One of a set or series of transformations of a theme (see THEME) by means of harmonic, rhythmic, and melodic changes and embellishments.

Varié (Fr., văh-rē-ā´). Varied. . . *Air* or *thème varié,* same as *Tema con variazioni.*

Varsovienne (Fr., var-sŏh-v'yen´). A dance in moderate tempo and ⅜ time, with an *Auftakt* of a quarter note, the downbeat of every second measure being strongly marked.

Vaudeville (Fr., voh-d'-vēl´). A comedy or parody in which dialogue and pantomime alternate with satirical couplets generally set to well-known popular airs.

Velato, -a (It., vĕh-lah´tŏh, -tăh). Veiled.

Veloce (It., vĕh-loh´chĕh). Rapid, swift; often means that a passage is to be performed faster than those before and after, then being the opposite of *ritenuto.*

Vent. (Fr., vahn). "Wind," as in *instruments à vent,* wind instruments.

Ventil. A valve.

Venusto (It., vĕh-nŏŏ´stŏh). Graceful, elegant.

Vergnügt (Ger., fâr-gnüyht´). Cheerful(ly), cheery (cheerily).

Vergrösserung (Ger., fâr-grös´serŏŏngᵏ). AUGMENTATION.

Verhallend (Ger., fâr-hähl´lent). Dying away.

Verismo (It., vĕr-ēz´mŏh). A realistic type of opera that emerged in Italy in the 1890s; its stories are based on contemporary fiction or actual dramatic events.

Verkleinerung (Ger., fâr-klīn´erŏŏngᵏ). See DIMINUTION.

116

Verlöschend (Ger., fâr-lö'shent). Dying away.

Vermindert (Ger., fâr-min'dert). Diminished (interval).

Verschiebung, mit (Ger., mit fâr-shē'bŏŏng^k). With soft pedal; *ohne Verschiebung*, release soft pedal.

Verschwindend (Ger., fâr-shvin'dent). Vanishing, dying away.

Verse. 1. In sacred vocal music, a portion of an anthem or service for a solo voice or solo voices.—2. A stanza.

Verse-anthem. One in which the verses predominate over the choruses. . . *Verse- service*, a choral service for solo voices.

Versetzung (Gcr., fâr-set'zŏŏng^k). Transposition.

Verweilend (Ger., fâr-vī'lent). Delaying.

Vespers. Evensong; the 6th of the Canonical Hours.

Vezzoso (It., vet-tsŏh'sŏh). In a graceful, elegant style.

Vibrante (It., vē-brăhn'tĕh). With a vibrating, agitated effect of tone.

Vibraphone. A percussion instrument consisting of suspended metal bars in keyboard arrangement, which, when struck with mallets, produce tones that are amplified by resonator tubes below the bars. A motor-driven mechanism causes the vibrato that gives the instrument its name.

Vibration. Rapid oscillations of a sounding body, such as a string, or a column of air in wind instruments, which result in the production of definite tones.

Vibrato (It., vē-brăh'tŏh). 1. On bowed instruments, the wavering effect of tone obtained by rapidly shaking the finger on the string which it is stopping.—2. In singing, *(a)* a tremulous effect caused by very rapid partial interruptions of the tone; *(b)* strongly accented, and diminishing intensity (also instrumental effect).

Vicendevole (It., vē-chen-dā'vŏh-lĕh). Changeably, inconstantly.

Vicino (It., vē-chē'nŏh). Near.

Vide (L., vī'deh). See. . . *Vi - - de*, written in scores, means that a "cut" is to be made, and directs the performers to skip from *Vi-* over to *de*.

Viel (Ger., fēl). Much, great. . . *Mit vielem Nachdruck*, with strong emphasis.

Vielle â roue (Fr., vē-ĕh'lĕh ăh roo). A medieval viol with a mechanical wheel attachment; a hurdy-gurdy.

Vielstimmig (Ger., fēl'shtim-mĭyh). Polyphonic, many-voiced.

Viennese school. Refers to various styles of composition centered around Austria. The *Classical Viennese School* includes Haydn, Mozart, Beethoven, Schubert, and others. The *20th Century Viennese School* refers to the group of composers, mainly Schoenberg and his disciples, who wrote in the DODECAPHONIC style.

Viertelnote (Ger., fĕr'tĕhl-noh-tĕh). A quarter note.

Vif (Fr., vēf). Lively.

Vigoroso (It., vē-gŏh-roh'sŏh). With vigor, energy.

Vihuela (Sp. bē-wĕh'lah). An old Spanish lute.

Villancico (Sp. bēl-yähn-sē'cŏh). A Spanish choral song of the Renaissance period.

Villanella (It., vēl-läh-nel'läh). Type of 16th-century vocal music originating in Naples and of a rather lighthearted nature, less refined than the madrigal.

Viol. A type of bowed instrument differing from the violin family by having a *fretted* fingerboard, a variable number of strings (usually 6), and in the shape of the body. It was made in 4 sizes, like the violin, by which it was superseded.

Viola (It., vē-ô'lah). The tenor violin. A bowed string instrument with its 4 strings tuned a fifth lower than the violin: *C, G, D, A.*

Viola da braccio (It., —brah'chŏh). Literally, "viol for the arm"; an old bowed string instrument held in the arm like the violin or viola.

Viola da gamba (It., —gahm'bäh). Literally, "viol for the leg"; an old bowed string instrument of the size approximating the cello, and held between the knees.

Viola d'amore (It., —däh-moh'rĕh). Literally, "a viola of love"; an ancient string instrument in the middle range, supplied with sympathetic strings.

Viole (Fr., v'yohl'). A viol; a viola.

Violin family. The familiar 4-stringed bowed instruments, constructed in 4 sizes, tuned as follows:

Violino (t., vē-ŏh-lē'nĕh). Violin.

Violon (Fr., v'yŏh-lŏhn'). Violin.

Violoncello (It., vē-ŏh-lŏhn-chel'lŏh). A 4-stringed bowed instrument of violin type, held, while playing, between the knees; familiarly called the 'cello.

Violone (It., vē-ŏh-loh'nŏh). The bass viol.

Virelai (Fr., vēr-eh-lā'). A medieval French song or ballad.

Virginal. A small kind of harpsichord.

Vista (It., vĭ´stăh). Slight. . . *A (prima) vista*, at (first) sight.

Visto, -a (It., vĭ´stŏh, -stăh). Briskly, animatedly.

Vite (Fr., veet). Fast.

Vivace (It., vē-vah´chĕh). Lively, animated, brisk. As a tempo mark standing by itself, *Vivace* calls for a movement equalling or exceedingly *Allegro* in rapidity.

Vivo (It., vē´vŏh). Lively, spiritedly, briskly.

Vocal. Pertaining to or suitable for the singing voice. . . *Vocal cords*, the 2 opposed ligaments set in the larynx, whose vibration, caused by expelling air from the lungs, produces vocal tones. . . *Vocal glottis*, the aperture between the vocal cords while singing.

Vocal score. An opera score arranged for voices and piano.

Vocalise (Fr., vŏh-căh-lēz´). A vocal exercise or etude, sung to the vowels or solmization syllables.

Voce (It., voh´chĕh). Voice; part.

Voce di petto (It., —dē pet´tŏh). Chest voice.

Voce di testa (It., —dē tes´tăh). Head voice.

Voice. The singing voice, divided into 6 principal classes: Soprano, Mezzo-soprano, Contralto (Alto), Tenor, Baritone, and Bass.

Voice leading. The art of arranging the voices in a polyphonic composition so that each part would have a logical continuation.

Voicing. Tuning (said of organ pipes).

Voix (Fr., v´wăh). Voice; part.

Volante (It., vŏh-lăhn´tĕh). Flying; light, swift.

Volkslied (Ger., fŏhlks´lē t). Folk song.

Volkstümlich (Ger., fŏhlks´tŭm´lĭyh). Like a German folk song, or popular music.

Voll (Ger., fŏhl). Full. . . *Volles Orchester*, full orchestra.

Volltönend (Ger., fŏhl-tön´ent). Sonorous, resonant.

Volta (t., vŏhl´tăh). A turn or time.

Volteggiando (It., vŏhl-ted-jăhn´dŏh). Crossing hands on a keyboard.

Volti subito (It., vŏhl´tē soo´bē-tŏh). Turn over instantly.

Volubilmente (It., vŏh-loo-bēl-men´tĕh). Fluently, flowingly.

Voluntary. An organ solo before, during, or after divine service, or, a choral piece opening the service.

Vom (Ger., fŏhm). From the. . . *Vom Anfang,* DA CAPO.

Vorausnahme (Ger., fohr-ows´nähme). See ANTICIPATION.

Vorhalt (Ger., fohr´hält). A suspension.

Vorher (Ger., fohr-här´). Before, previous(ly).

Vorig (Ger., fohr´iyh). Preceding, previous; as *voriges Zeitmass (tempo precedente).*

Vorschlag (Ger., fohr´shläyh). See APPOGGIATURA.

Vorspiel (Ger., fohr´shpēl). Prelude, introduction; overture.

Vortrag (Ger., fohr´trah). Rendering, interpretation, performance, style, execution.

Vortragszeichen (Ger., fohr´trah-tsīh-en). Expression mark.

Vorwärts (Ger., fohr´värts). Forward; *etwas vorwärts gehend,* somewhat faster.

Vox (L. vôx). Voice. . . *Vox humana* (human voice), an 8´ reed stop in the organ.

Vuoto, -a (It., voo-oh´toh, -täh). "Empty"; used in the indication *corda vuota,* "open string."

W

Wachsend (Ger., väh´sent). Crescendo, "growing."

Wagner tuba. A brass instrument introduced by Wagner in his music dramas, in two sizes, tenor and bass.

Waldhorn (Ger., vähl´horn). The French horn without valves.

Waltz. A round dance in ¾ time, varying in tempo from slow to moderately fast.

Walzer (Ger., vähl´tser). Waltz.

Wehmüt(h)ig (Ger., vä´mü´tïyh). In a style expressive of sadness or melancholoy.

Weich (Ger., vīyh). Soft, tender; mellow, suave.

Weichnachtsmusik (Ger., vī´nahts-moo-zĭk). Christmas music.

Well tempered. In equal temperament, as in Bach's *Well Tempered Clavier.*

Wenig (Ger., vä´nĭyh). Little; *ein klein wenig langsamer,* a very little slower.

Whipping bow. A form of violin technique in which the bow is made to fall with a certain vehemence on the strings.

White note. One with an open head: (𝅗𝅥𝅗𝅥).

Whole note. The note 𝅝.

Whole shift. See SHIFT.

Whole step. 1. The step of a whole tone.—2. A whole tone.

Whole tone. A major Second.

Whole-tone scale. A scale consisting only of whole tones, and therefore lacking the dominant and either major or minor triads.

Wie (Ger., vē). As.—*Wie oben,* as above; *wie vorher,* as before, as at first.

Wiegend (Ger., vē´ghent). Swaying, rocking.

Wiegenlied (Ger., vee´ghen-leed). A lullaby.

Wind band. 1. A company of performers on wind instruments.—2. The wind instruments in the orchestra; also, the players on, or parts written for, the same.

Wind instruments. Instruments whose tones are produced by compressed air.

Wolf. 1. The discord produced when playing, in certain keys, on an organ tuned in unequal temperament.—2. In bowed instruments, an imperfect or jarring vibration caused by sounding some particular tone or tones.

Wood block. Another name for temple block.

Woodwind. Wind instruments that use reeds (clarinet, oboe, saxophone, etc.) and the flute (which formerly was made of wood and, in the recorder, still is).

Working-out. Development section in sonata form.

Wuchtig (Ger., vŏŏh´tĭyh). Weighty, weightily, ponderous(ly), with strong emphasis.

Würdevoll (Ger., vür´dĕ-fŏhl´). With dignity; loftily.

Wüt(h)end (Ger., vü´tent). Furious(ly), frantic(ally).

X

Xylophone. A percussion instrument consisting of a row of flat wooden bars fastened horizontally to two stretched cords, tuned to the tones of the scale, and struck with two mallets.

Y

Yodel. A type of singing in Switzerland and other Alpine regions, characterized by the frequent alternation of falsetto tones with chest tones.

Z

Zapateado (Sp., thăh-păh-tā-ăh´dŏ). Spanish dance in triple time, characterized by heel stamping to emphasize the strong syncopation.

Zart (Ger., tsăhrt). Tender, soft, delicate, *dolce*; slender.

Zärtlich (Ger., tsärt´lĭyh). Tender(ly), caressing(ly).

Zarzuela (Sp. thăhr-thoo-āl´ăh). Type of Spanish opera with spoken dialogue.

Zeitmass (Ger., tzīt´măhs). Tempo.

Zeloso (It., dzĕh-loh´sŏh). Zealously, enthusiastically, with energy and fire.

Ziemlich (Ger., tsēm´lĭyh). Neat(ly), delicate(ly); graceful(ly).

Zigeunermusik (Ger., tsĭ-goy´ner-moo-zĭk). Gypsy music.

Zither (Ger., tsit´ter). A string instrument with 32 or more strings stretched over a shallow wooden resonance box and having a fretted fingerboard on the side next the player; above the fingerboard are 5 melody strings, plucked with a metal "ring" worn on the right thumb.

Zitternd (Ger., tsit´ternt). Trembling, tremulous.

Zögernd (Ger., tsö´gernt). Hesitating, retarding.

Zu (Ger., tsoo). Too; to.

Zunehmend (Ger., tsoo´nā´ment). Increasing, *crescendo*.

Zurückhaltend (Ger., tsoo-rük´hähl´tent). Holding back, *ritardando*.

Zwei (Ger., tsvī). Two.

Zweihändig (Ger., tsvī´hen´dĭyh). For 2 hands.

Zweistimmig (Ger., tsvī´shtim´mĭyh). For 2 voices; in or for 2 parts.

Zwischensatz (Ger., tsvish´en-zăhts´). Episode.

Zwischenspiel (Ger., tsvish´en-shpēl´). Interlude, intermezzo.